DIVERSITY IN THE CLASSROOM:
A CASEBOOK FOR TEACHERS AND TEACHER EDUCATORS

Edited by

Judith H. Shulman

and

Amalia Mesa-Bains

of

The Far West Laboratory for Educational

Research and Development

Published collaboratively by Research for Better Schools and Lawrence Erlbaum Associates

Lawrence Erlbaum Associates, Inc., Publishers
365 Broadway
Hillsdale, New Jersey 07642

Library of Congress Cataloging-in-Publication Data

Diversity in the classroom : a casebook for teachers and teacher
  educators / edited by Judith H. Shulman and Amalia Mesa-Bains.
      p.   cm.
    Includes bibliographical references (p.   ).
    ISBN 0-8058-1428-0. -- ISBN 0-8058-1429-9 (pbk.)
    1. Minorities--Education--United States--Case studies.
  2. Multicultural education--United States--Case studies.
  I. Shulman, Judith. II. Mesa-Bains, Amalia.
  LC3731.D59 1993
  371.97'0973--dc20   93-22948
                                          CIP

Work on this publication was supported in part by the U.S. Department of Education, Office of Educational Research
and Improvement, contract number RP91002006 and RP91002004. Its contents do not necessarily reflect the views of the
Department of Education.

Books published by Lawrence Erlbaum Associates are printed on acid-free paper, and their
bindings are chosen for strength and durability.

Printed in the United States of America

10 9 8 7 6 5 4 3 2

DIVERSITY IN THE CLASSROOM:
A CASEBOOK FOR TEACHERS AND TEACHER EDUCATORS

Editors:

Judith H. Shulman
and
Amalia Mesa-Bains

Far West Laboratory

Case Writers:

Josephine Arce
Linda Dmytriw
Judy Drummond
Audrey Fielding
Gil Guillermo

Bette Mohr
Lori Murakami
Peg Foley Reynolds
Lilly Siu
Terrie St. Michel

Anna Yamaguchi
Lynne Zolli

Commentators:

Carne Barnett
Larry Cuban
Karen Desser
Diane Garfield
Bettye Haysbert
Christine Hiroshima
Beverly Jimenez
Alice Kawazoe

Gloria Ladson-Billings
Joel Littauer
Morgan Marchbanks
Amalia Mesa-Bains
Lois Meyer
Lori Murakami
Sharon Nelson-Barber
Amado Padilla

Richard Piper
Michi Pringle
Heather Ramirez
Peg Foley Reynolds
Lilly Siu
Joan Tibbetts
Anna Yamaguchi
Lynne Zolli

Published collaboratively by Research for Better Schools and Lawrence Erlbaum Associates

LIST OF CONTRIBUTORS

Josephine Arce, Teacher, San Francisco Unified School District

Carne Barnett, Mathematics Educator, Far West Laboratory

Larry Cuban, Professor, Stanford University

Karen Desser, Teacher, San Mateo Union High School District

Linda Dmytriw, Teacher, Los Angeles Unified School District

Judy Drummond, Teacher, San Francisco Unified School District

Audrey Fielding, English Coordinator/ACCESS, University of California, Berkeley

Diane Garfield, Teacher, San Francisco Unified School District

Gil Guillermo, Teacher, San Francisco Unified School District

Bettye Haysbert, Staff Developer, San Francisco Unified School District

Christine Hiroshima, Staff Developer, San Francisco Unified School District

Beverly Jimenez, Consulting Principal, Achievement Council/San Francisco Unified School District

Alice Kawazoe, Director, Staff Development & Curriculum, Oakland Unified School District

Gloria Ladson-Billings, Assistant Professor, University of Wisconsin

Joel Littauer, Teacher, Los Angeles Unified School District

Morgan Marchbanks, Teaching Fellow, Stanford University

Amalia Mesa-Bains, Educational Scholar/Staff Developer, Far West Laboratory/San Francisco Unified School District

Lois Meyer, Assistant Professor, San Francisco State University

Bette Mohr, Teacher, Phoenix Union High School District

Lori Murakami, Teacher, San Francisco Unified School District

Sharon Nelson-Barber, Assistant Professor, Stanford University

Amado Padilla, Professor of Education, Stanford University

Richard Piper, Director, California Learning Designs, Inc.

Michi Pringle, Staff Developer, San Francisco Unified School District

Heather Ramirez, Teaching Fellow, Stanford University

Peg Foley Reynolds, Teacher, San Francisco Unified School District

Judith Shulman, Director, Institute for Case Development, Far West Laboratory

Lilly Siu, Teacher, San Francisco Unified School District

Terrie St. Michel, Teacher, Phoenix Union High School District

Joan Tibbetts, Teacher, San Francisco Unified School District

Anna Yamaguchi, Teacher, San Francisco Unified School District

Lynne Zolli, Teacher, San Francisco Unified School District

TABLE OF CONTENTS

FOREWORD

Far West Laboratory for Educational Research and
Development (FWL) is a non-profit agency dedicated to
improving the quality of education by helping policy-
makers and practitioners apply the best available
knowledge from research, development, and practice. A
federally designated regional laboratory funded in part
by the U.S. Department of Education, FWL addresses a
broad range of educational priorities, including issues of
early childhood, students at risk, assessment and ac-
countability, educational technology, and professional
development.

This volume joins *The Mentor Teacher Casebook* and *The
Intern Teacher Casebook* as the latest in the pioneering
series of teacher-written casebooks being developed by
our Institute for Case Development. Other publications
focus on administrators, middle schools, and mathematics teaching. All are aimed at helping bridge the gap
between theory and practice in preparing practitioners
for a work environment where there are few clear right
or wrong courses of action.

By focusing on the enormous new diversity in today's
classrooms, this book aims to help teachers find answers
to challenges they face as they struggle to meet the needs
of all students.

Dean Nafziger
Executive Director
Far West Laboratory

PREFACE

This volume is the third in a series of casebooks developed at the Far West Laboratory (FWL). These casebooks are part of a nationwide effort to capture and use practitioner knowledge to better prepare teachers for the reality of today's classrooms.

Unlike business, law, and medicine, education has made little formal use of cases as professional training tools. But interest in case-based teaching is now growing in both teacher preparation and inservice training programs. The 1980s reform movement is largely responsible. In the effort to improve schools, it's become clear that teachers are woefully unprepared for the huge array of challenges presented by a student population vastly different from that of even a decade ago. Novices find the gritty, real-life classroom to be light years from the ideal they had imagined as students. Spotlighting this gap between theory and practice, the 1986 Carnegie report, *A Nation Prepared: Teachers for the 21st Century*, recommended that teacher training institutions use "cases illustrating a great variety of teaching problems" as "a major focus of instruction."

What do we mean by cases? Cases are candid, dramatic, highly readable accounts of teaching events or series of events. They show a problem-based snapshot of an on-the-job dilemma. Read alone, they offer the vicarious experience of walking in another's shoes. But in group discussion, they are especially powerful, allowing differing points of view to be aired and examined. For that reason, cases are consciously designed to provoke discussion that is engaging, demanding, intellectually exciting, and stimulating.

Some cases are written by researchers. But those we have pioneered over the past five years at FWL are written by teachers themselves. They are also coupled with commentaries written by other teachers, administrators, or educational scholars whose different, often conflicting, interpretations of the narrative provide additional lenses through which to view the case.

Because they tell vivid, moving stories, cases give life and staying power to concepts. Teacher educators, mentors and staff developers are using cases to trigger discussion about why a given strategy works or doesn't. Beginners learn from experienced teachers how to create lessons and environments that promote learning. They learn how to frame problems, interpret complex situations, and identify decision points and possible consequences — that is, they learn to think like teachers. So veterans discuss teaching situations that mirror their own, in the process reflecting on their values, attitudes, and assumptions and wrestling with the disequilibrium this creates. As a result, they often change their beliefs about teaching and learning and, thus, adopt very different ways of working with students.

FAR WEST LABORATORY'S APPROACH

The FWL case writing process makes practitioners themselves the subjects, producers, and consumers of action research. We emphasize this because teachers generally have few mechanisms to record and preserve their accumulated knowledge. When a teacher retires or otherwise leaves the profession, his or her understanding, methods, and materials — which should form a legacy to the profession, the community, and the school — are generally lost. Today, however, there is an expanding literature on the practitioner experience. The casebooks contribute to it by combining the growing body of research about teaching with specific accounts of classroom dilemmas written by teachers themselves.

But cases are not simply narrative descriptions of events. To call something a case is to make a theoretical claim — that it is a case *of* something, or an instance of a larger class. For example, an account of a teacher observing a colleague teach a lesson and later engaging that colleague in an analysis of the lesson is a case of coaching.

Cases may also be exemplars of principles, describing by their detail a general pattern of practice.

All the narratives in our casebooks meet this criterion. They are selected because they represent a larger class of experiences. In our first volume, *The Mentor Teacher Casebook*, 22 mentor teachers from the Los Angeles Unified School District (LAUSD) describe the rewards and frustrations of providing on-the-job assistance to beginning teachers. An outgrowth of our study of the California Mentor Teacher Program's first year, its vignettes describe how the mentor-colleague relationship develops and illustrate the complexity of the new mentor role. In the second casebook *(The Intern Teacher Casebook)* first-year teachers — again in LAUSD — describe in frank and moving detail the reality shock they experienced during their first few months instructing teenagers in inner-city schools. Their stories frequently reveal their initial inability to understand youngsters with backgrounds radically different from their own. They also portray the enormous challenge of simultaneously encountering two new cultures: teaching and poverty.

ABOUT THIS CASEBOOK

The 13 cases in the pages that follow are again set in diverse, inner-city schools. But this time they are written by outstanding veteran teachers who describe some of the most problematic experiences of their careers. Some look back to their novice days, describe how they handled a situation, and reflect on what they might do differently now. Others tell about current problems and leave us with unresolved dilemmas.

These cases were developed collaboratively by a researcher from FWL, a staff developer/researcher from the San Francisco Unified School District (SFUSD), and 11 teachers nominated by their peers as excellent. These teachers all work with ethnically and culturally diverse youngsters: eight at the elementary level, one at a junior high, and two in high schools. Their own varied ethnic backgrounds include Japanese-American, Chinese-American, Latino, Filipino, and Caucasian. Eight teach in SFUSD, two in the Phoenix Unified School District, and one in LAUSD.

The commentaries that follow each case are intended to broaden case analysis rather than to answer unresolved questions. They purposely offer differing interpretations of the case, raise critical questions, and explore issues that are either overt or suggested by nuances in the narrative. Some commentators link their remarks to scholarly articles to bridge the gap between theory and practice. Others write more subjective comments or tell stories of their own. Like the authors, the commentators come from backgrounds that are ethnically and professionally diverse. This was deliberate, since we wanted perspectives that would enrich, not simplify, analysis and understanding of about the issues embedded in the cases.

TIPS FOR USING THESE CASES

This book is for use in preservice and inservice multicultural education courses. It aims to help new and experienced teachers become more aware of and understand the ethnic, racial, and cultural expressions of the diverse students in their classrooms. As you read the cases, we hope you will begin to examine your own perceptions and attitudes, just as we have examined ours during the process of creating this volume. We also hope that the cases will prompt you to think about different ways of teaching that might enable you to better relate classroom activities to your particular students and tailor instruction to their needs.

As stated above, cases are powerful discussion catalysts. Good discussion can help people dig into a case. What did this teacher actually do and why? With what result? What alternative strategies might have been tried? At what risk? Did the cultural perceptions of the teacher or students influence the situation? How do you know? What were students thinking and feeling? How did they try to communicate this to the teacher? Does this teacher's story parallel experiences of your own? Has this session led you to think of different ways of handling these dilemmas?

An *Instructor's Guide* is being prepared to accompany this casebook. It includes questions specific to each case along with additional background. Discussions sprung from such questions can help people to: 1) spot issues and frame problems in ambiguous situations, 2) interpret situations from different perspectives, 3) identify crucial decision points and possibilities for action, 4) recognize the possible consequences of different actions, and 5) identify and/or test teaching principles in real classroom situations.

The commentaries add information and insights participants might otherwise not have. Those in this book are particularly useful when the discussion group doesn't include a real cultural mix. The commentators then function as cultural informants, providing background essential to meaningful discussion, whether about realities of life in urban housing projects or the marginalization of minority teachers. Depending on the situation and group goals, commentaries may be read with the case or introduced after an initial discussion as the basis for second-stage analysis.

ACKNOWLEDGMENTS

We would first like to thank the case writers for taking time out of their busy schedules to write such interesting and candid accounts. These teachers had the courage to both question their beliefs and document their perceptions through multiple drafts of their cases. Thanks to the commentators who stretched our thinking by providing their perspectives to each case. Thanks also to Don Barfield and Carne Barnett of Far West Laboratory, and Linda Davis, Deputy Superintendent for Instruction at the San Francisco Unified School District and member of FWL's Board of Directors, who supported and guided this project from its inception. We are also indebted to our advisors Sharon Nelson-Barber, Amado Padilla, and Lee Shulman of Stanford University, and Gloria Ladson-Billings of the University of Wisconsin, who wrote commentaries, provided wise insights, and asked difficult questions.

Several other individuals made valuable contributions: Judith Kleinfeld, University of Alaska, Fairbanks, and William McDiarmid, Michigan State University, gave us input on drafts; Joan McRobbie, our talented editor and number one supporter, helped us through several revisions; Leslie Crenna helped develop the annotated bibliography; and Rosemary De La Torre patiently typed and revised multiple drafts and designed the book's initial version, and Fredrika Baer provided desktop publishing.

Judith H. Shulman
Amalia Mesa-Bains

INTRODUCTION

*The Context
of Cultural
Diversity*

Amalia Mesa-Bains

Today's startling classroom diversity reflects a major U.S. demographic shift. The greatest wave of immigration since the turn of the century, combined with escalating birth rates, is creating a society with no distinct majority—one characterized by multicultural enclaves in many cities and rural areas. The student population in these areas is enormously mixed, encompassing an array of races, cultures, and languages never before seen in single schools or classrooms. Teachers face multiple and complex issues that challenge many of their educational practices and assumptions. For example, majority-minority relations, long a focus of concern in urban classrooms, are at very least reconfigured and may, in fact, be moot. In many schools there is no longer a majority group; in others, the traditional white dominant, black minority nature of the racial composition may instead be Latino-black or Chinese-Latino.

Teachers must understand students' home lives, too. The hardships faced by youngsters in urban housing projects, for example, or the struggles between generations in otherwise strong immigrant families profoundly influence a student's motivation and ability to succeed in school. Moreover, the cultural norms students bring from home add new subtleties to such issues as those stemming from class and gender.

The cases in this book are set in San Francisco, Los Angeles, and Phoenix, three of the nation's most diverse cities. The teacher-authors tell of classroom dilemmas so complex that even choosing terms to describe them is difficult. Words like multicultural, while useful, don't convey certain deeper realities of race and class or critical distinctions among ethnicity, nationality, culture, and citizenship. Moreover, the attempt to speak candidly can run headlong into accusations of stereotyping. When we piloted this casebook with groups of teachers, we realized that some of its cases, particularly those dealing with bias, race, and class, generated heated interchange and ran the risk of polarizing opinions and creating defensive assumptions.

These topics *can* be talked about with candor and civility, however. And candid discussion is vital, since race, cultural behaviors, and socioeconomic circumstance have important implications for classroom practices. By examining such issues we begin to see the need for a greater variety of teaching styles, distribution of opportunities, and educational access for all students.

GROWING SOCIOECONOMIC CONCERNS

One of the most alarming statistics about America's changing demographics is that the poorest 20 percent of the population is able to earn and use only 4.5 percent of the nation's wealth. The growing gap between the haves and have nots has created a true underclass. This group's struggles for social and economic survival underlie many of the cases in this book. That survival is linked to how students fare in school, and that, in turn, is influenced both by teacher perceptions and students' own expectations.

For example, many teachers are influenced by unconscious notions about black students. These stem in part from media coverage that tends to emphasize crime and violence in the black community. Though events reported are real, the preponderance of negative news stories often distorts the public image of African-Americans. Students in low income communities, meanwhile, particularly those living in housing projects, are conditioned by their limited opportunities and day-to-day hardships to expect little benefit from education.

This powerful interpenetration of race and class has created among some a sense of disenfranchisement. Since schools perpetuate the myth of a classless society, students' socioeconomic class is rarely acknowledged as a factor in educational achievement.

NEEDS OF IMMIGRANT CHILDREN

Other dilemmas these cases depict are rooted in the problems faced by newly arrived immigrant families. For Latinos with historic ties to the Southwestern Territory and Mexico, immigration and internal colonization are key aspects of community ancestry and current reality. Many of our Mexican and Central American children are coming from areas so rural or so torn by civil strife that no consistent, ongoing education has been provided in over a generation. This educational deficit is coupled with extreme economic deprivation, affecting health and well-being. Ironically, even the journey of escape and migration to a better life brings more difficulties for many students. Separation, culture shock, loss, exposure to violence, and limited English proficiency often combine to create a kind of post-traumatic stress syndrome. Some children exhibit a lack of interest or low affect as a result of overwhelming circumstances.

Clearly, many of our incoming students are not school-ready. Even Asian students, so-called model minorities, may struggle against barriers to learning. Inherent in Chinese, Japanese, Korean, and Indochinese communities are intercultural conflicts stemming from the colonial experience and past territorial aggressions. Large numbers of Chinese immigrants have come from areas with strong, long standing educational systems. Often the educational and professional accomplishments of their family members contribute to overly high achievement expectations, causing pressures that affect these children's emotional well-being. Though established economic improvement networks often make the Asian socio-economic situation different from that of many Latin Americans, many Indochinese students entering our schools are also beset by post-traumatic stress, limited English proficiency, and culture shock.

SCHOOL DISTRICT REALITIES: COURT ORDERS AND STATE MANDATES

All three school districts participating in these cases— Los Angeles, Phoenix, and San Francisco—struggle to meet the needs of growing multilingual populations while maintaining broad-based commitments to integrating schools and classrooms. The San Francisco Unified School District (SFUSD) faces the dilemma of accommodating two court orders, one requiring special language support, the other desegregation.

The services and approaches that the courts have mandated for SFUSD must be carefully orchestrated so that self-contained bilingual classes do not contradict schoolwide efforts at integration. Consequently, many schools have sought to integrate special language support activities for portions of the day. Besides language and desegregation demands, the district must offer programs addressing the needs of gifted and talented, special education, and below-grade-level students.

This complicated system of resources and mandates is but one factor urban teachers must manage as they try to provide appropriate and meaningful classroom learning experiences for all students.

TEACHERS' NEED FOR MULTICULTURAL EDUCATION

More fundamentally, many teachers have had no sustained contact with individuals of another race prior to entering the inner-city classroom. Not only do they lack familiarity; most are fearful of confronting the issue of race at all. In college they had been taught that "blacks were really the same as white people, except perhaps they were culturally deprived."

Such teachers clearly need inservice programs in multicultural education. A number of districts provide such programs based on a traditional model—teachers learn instructional strategies that accommodate and take advantage of differences in values, experiences, and beliefs. But experience at SFUSD suggests that this is not enough; the relationship between teacher and student involves not just instruction but interaction. When interaction fails because of teacher misperceptions of student behavior, instructional failure often follows.

So the district has created an "interactional" staff development program. Not only a new model, it in fact introduces a new paradigm for multicultural programs. In its sessions, teachers discuss race and class issues openly, reflect on previously held views about different cultures, and confront their own prejudices and stereotypes. Examining their own perceptions has allowed teachers to begin truly absorbing and using cultural information about their students' learning styles.

Because of desegregation mandates, the emphasis in SFUSD's training is on cultural diversity, primarily in curriculum areas such as social studies/history and language arts. The program presents a general overview of cultural learning styles and strategies that support them.

As implementation has evolved, the training has become more site-based and more relevant to specific school settings and particular student populations. Teachers have gained an awareness of how teacher expectations influence student achievement, and they are learning strategies for cooperative learning and conflict resolution. Now they want help in adapting what they learn to their individual classroom realities. Rather than dealing only in generalities, e.g., talking of blacks, Latinos, Asians, or limited English speakers in terms of broad cultural knowledge or sets of characteristics, teachers need specific classroom scenarios that they can analyze and use as the basis for problem solving. Otherwise, the learning that takes place — whether it be in cultural understanding, human relations, or anti-racism — is disembodied and easily forgotten.

How Cases Can Help

Case-based teaching can help. Cases provide a bridge between the general topic and specific practices. Within a multicultural program, the case approach can serve as a distancing mechanism, allowing majority and minority teachers to talk together about issues ordinarily too difficult to discuss openly. Our experience using case methods in mentor training showed us how effective this approach can be.

Cases prompt reflection and personal involvement. They allow teachers like those in SFUSD to examine large-scale problems close up. Cases introduce us to a particular student and teacher, bringing the world of one classroom to life in all its complexity. Problems under discussion are no longer those of, say, poor black children, but of Eric, a very memorable, very real little boy with feelings, talents, and family members. His needs may or may not be "typical," but his teacher tries to meet them in the best way she and her school can. Those reading and discussing the case use the situation as a vehicle for questioning their own instructional practices, classroom management strategies, and multicultural curriculum and for reflecting on their own values, attitudes, and experience. Information in the case is supplemented by other curriculum materials, e.g., a model that offers specific steps for handling disruptive classroom behavior or training in cooperative learning strategies. The case, in other words, functions as the hub of the staff development wheel.

The following cases are part of a nationwide case development momentum. Like all good stories, they don't necessarily end neatly with success and resolution. Instead, the teacher is often left puzzled, wondering if his or her interventions could have been better or more thoughtful. By prompting questioning and reflection and enabling differing points of view to be expressed and explored, they can truly be catalysts for teacher change.

CHAPTER 1

Teaching New Concepts and Skills

Introducing new ideas and supporting learners in new curriculum areas is difficult under any circumstances. But when teachers are unfamiliar with the culturally diverse backgrounds of their students, their frustration is heightened by uncertainty about succeeding at basic communication. Teacher-student interaction figures profoundly into the teaching of new concepts and skills. The three cases in this section draw our attention to how cultural realities affect that interaction. They depict three different learning situations and cultural contexts.

In **A Case of Ganas**, the story of Amparo conveys a teacher's sense of failure while paradoxically revealing the student's new understanding of her own learning. The backdrop for this moving student-teacher relationship is the student's cultural history, community experiences, and family values. The commentaries allow us to view the same narrative from several perspectives and to challenge the teacher's perception of her ineffectiveness.

Moments of Truth: Teaching *Pygmalion* is set in a dynamic African-American community. The teacher finds that issues of language and social status confuse and cloud her genuine attempts to introduce a new approach to an old classic. Whether she missed an opportunity for deeper student engagement is a question debated in the commentaries.

Finally, in **Attempting to Teach Self-Esteem**, a teacher's idealistic efforts to resolve problems of poverty and self-esteem fall flat. This case allows us to reflect on how well-meaning lessons can go awry if they fail to recognize and accommodate students' developmental needs.

Case 1

A Case of Ganas[1]

When Amparo asked me to help her write a book for the Young Author's Contest, I braced myself. She couldn't spell, had no idea of sentence boundaries, and didn't recognize — let alone abide by — the rules of standard usage. It wasn't that she spelled phonetically, because she didn't; even phonetic spelling follows patterns of sound. Amparo wrote in a gibberish all her own.

Amparo wasn't dumb. She could organize pages of ideas with astounding fluency. However, the absence of paragraph indentations coupled with gross syntactical reversions and omissions resulted in writing that approached incomprehensibility. Amparo was a problem. Just reading what she wrote took up too much time.

On the other hand, Amparo was gifted with ideas. She could analyze and put together concepts. She wasn't loquacious, but when she talked she made sense. I liked Amparo and wanted to help her out. I think she had a processing problem, maybe dyslexia. English wasn't her first language, yet that didn't completely explain her plight. She'd lived in the U. S. for years. I think her reading skills were low, but so were most everyone else's. In my junior high, the average reading level was fourth grade. There were gaps of information regarding Amparo's prior experience in school. By the middle of the second semester her cumulative folder still hadn't arrived. She had missed my own screening because she entered the classroom a few weeks into the year.

I'd hoped Amparo would pair up with another student to write her book for the contest, but she wanted to do her own. When students pair up, there are fewer works to grade, edit, assemble, and bind. While other students chose to work on romances, poetry, and adventures, I suggested to Amparo that she develop an essay she'd

_____

[1]At their request, the authors of individual cases will remain anonymous. In addition, pseudonyms have been used for all names and places found within the narratives.

already done into a longer piece. "Yes, Miss," she said, "I want to do that, but I don't know how."

In many ways Amparo is typical of a small group of hard-working junior high school girls in East Los Angeles who haven't had a lot of academic success. She has a rather timid version of *ganas*, or a desire to do well, yet she feels she can't. And she knows there's something "wrong" with the way her thoughts come out on paper. It's as if she has a writer's temperament but seriously lacks skills. Mostly, she likes to carefully copy poems. Like many students who have been through "too much" ineffective remediation, Amparo is turned off to meaningless drill and exercise.

The essay Amparo decided to expand was originally titled, "My Family and the One I Hope to Have Someday." In the end, we changed it to "My Family and the American Ideal: An Ethnographic Composition." In class we'd already gone through some rather technical newspaper articles on families throughout the U. S. A. and had many lively class discussions. We broke the words "ethnographic" and "composition" into prefixes, suffixes, and roots and began with autobiographical incidents. Amparo was able to formulate generalizations about families and compare her own to others in her community and the country. Writing for her was like hanging beautiful fabrics on the more pleasant cognitive hooks of her mind. Although she referred to the negative aspects of her community, she preferred not to dwell on those problems.

The most stressful part of this project for me was dealing with all the frustrations she had in producing a clean final draft. I simply didn't have time to try a deductive approach to error correction. Sometimes I re-wrote her sentences for her. Other times I couldn't even do that without asking her for a "translation." Peer-editing, in this project, wasn't effective. I'd already given her permission to work alone. Because she insisted on typing, new errors emerged. These typed pages again had to be edited. At home, only Amparo's little sister and brother spoke English. Twice I didn't get around to proofreading her work overnight and she panicked. I felt for her anxiety yet I had 150 other students to deal with every day.

In the end, Amparo just made the deadline. The pink fabric paint on the turquoise cloth cover was still damp as she handed her paper in to the judges. To our delight, the book was among those chosen to represent our school in the district exhibit.

I have mixed feelings when I think back on my experiences with Amparo. It was she who taught me about her family and the community to which it belonged:

> My mother is understanding, caring, and kind. My father withdraws his love and trust if you do something wrong or disappoint him in some undesirable way. My uncles are always there. In many ways we are almost like our neighbors. We are Mexican-American. Our neighborhood has lovely fashion shops and restaurants that are built well. Mother would prefer living in some more peaceful place with less troublemakers, but my father prefers East L. A. because of his friends. We are a loving family. We are Catholic. In Church the Father uses these words that just make you think about what has happened to you. In a way, you change the way you are or at least the way you think about others.

Perhaps her most haunting passage was,

> In my other school something bothered me. I used to think that I was not good because they had me in a special class. They did a good job in a way but I used to be afraid I was dumb. Now the teachers really try to teach us what they know and they're good at that.

Here I'm afraid Amparo was wrong. I never did learn how to effectively "correct" serious composition prob-

lems that prevented her from being fully literate. She may have thought I was a good teacher but I wasn't good enough. Amparo was diligent and smart, yet subsequent writing from her showed serious mechanical problems were still there. We were back to gibberish. I am faced with that gnawing frustration of having won the battle but lost a war. What, I ask myself, can an inner-city barrio school teacher do to more effectively deal with all those Amparos who truly want to learn, who have a timid yet desperate case of *ganas*?

Amado M. Padilla
Stanford University

In its formal usage, the word *ganas* in Spanish means to desire or want. In other words, it suggests the motivational level of the individual. However, in barrio Spanish it also has the connotation of a challenge. In this account, there are two challenges being addressed. In the obvious one, Amparo wants to produce a book for the contest. She knows that she has problems in writing. Yet she has the courage to want to write a book and, moreover, to do it alone except for the teacher's help. It would be so much easier to either not have the *ganas* to do a book at all or to team up with another student. Amparo, however, reaches down into the essence of her being and draws the strength to persist in her desire to do the book. In the process she challenges the teacher by implicitly asking, "Do you have the *ganas* to help me? " To me, the interesting question is, why did the teacher accept the challenge?

The teacher knew that it would be tough to work with Amparo. Yet the teacher agreed and rationalized it by saying, "I liked Amparo and wanted to help her out." I believe that this too altruistic sounding statement is not the real reason why the teacher helped Amparo. I submit that the teacher recognized in Amparo's plea a challenge. Thus, it is the teacher's *ganas* that is really being discussed in this vignette.

We learn how time consuming and frustrating it is to teach barrio youngsters who come to school from poor and non-English speaking homes, regardless of how much *ganas* they may have to learn. After all, as the teacher stated, Amparo was not the only student. There were in fact another 150 students! I believe that Amparo will for a very long time appreciate and remember the help she received from her teacher. She was, after all, amply rewarded. The teacher accepted her challenge and, more important, followed through to the end by helping her produce a book. Moreover, her book was selected to represent the school in the district exhibit.

But, will the teacher remember the experience in the same positive way that Amparo most likely will?

Amparo may eventually learn to write because she has the *ganas* to do so and because of this single positive experience with a teacher who cared. Who knows, someday Amparo could win a Pulitzer Prize. However, will the teacher survive long enough to accept another challenge from one of the many hundreds of barrio youngsters like Amparo? How long will the teacher last in education before thinking about life after teaching and getting that real estate license?

Teaching in the barrio requires more *ganas* than most teachers have or even care to have. Yet if Hispanic students like Amparo are to join the mainstream of society, teachers must look beyond the superficial mechanical errors that these students make in the use of English and recognize the burning desire that so many have of wanting to learn. To do this, though, a teacher needs a very deep well of *ganas* because there are hundreds of Amparos in every barrio school.

Joel Littauer, Teacher
Los Angeles Unified School District

Ordinarily, a problem that falls within the realm of the typical is an easy one to solve. Not so in teaching. The case under study is typical because it has not been solved. Worse yet, no solution appears on the educational horizon.

The conditions under which this East Los Angeles teacher must work actually militate against recognizable accomplishment of any sort. One hundred fifty students a day means an average class size of 30. Moreover, many students are, like Amparo, non-native English speakers. As the teacher observes, Amparo's difficulties may be further complicated by dyslexia. This perceptual difficulty likely went undetected, in which case the child was not taught compensatory skills. Starting thus from behind, the teacher needs more than the standard 40- to 60-minute teaching period daily to have an impact on students like Amparo. Individual tutoring beyond the school day would seem to be indicated.

Many teachers begin their careers highly charged with *ganas*. Too often, *ganas* is beaten to death by years of unrealized goals. *Ganas* is sapped and replaced by a lassitude that waits for a bell to ring and something miraculous to happen. Lacking such a miracle, young teachers escape into other areas such as real estate or the law, while older teachers simply bide their time until retirement. Amado M. Padilla has written eloquently of the predicament of the classroom teacher: uncertainty regarding self worth and a need to reinforce that worth even if it means leaving the teaching profession — and too often that is exactly what it means.

What is the solution? The teacher in this case apparently hasn't found a long-range answer. The short-term answer was to edit Amparo's book for her — a Band-Aid response. But the teacher is left with nagging doubts. How much had Amparo really been helped? After all, Amparo's composition technique had not noticeably improved. Mr. Padilla may be correct: Amparo may one day win a Pulitzer Prize. After all, it is in the nature of our profession that the best we can offer our students is deferred gratification. But the corollary to that is that the teacher's gratification is also deferred. We must wait until our students come back to us and tell us of the prizes they have won, and how our courses were the determining factor in their successes.

What can be offered to our teacher is faith — and study. If education can satisfy a student's *ganas*, perhaps it can satisfy a teacher's as well. Continue to study teaching methods. Join study groups such as the California Writing Project. The answer may not come immediately, but eventually it must come. And when it does, a teacher with true *ganas* will recognize it. Don't despair. Keep teaching. Amparo needs you. All the Amparos need you.

Alice Kawazoe, Staff Development & Curriculum Director
Oakland Unified School District

"Mostly she likes to carefully copy poems." To carefully copy poems is a simple and safe act, like tracing a drawing, ensuring a mistake-free, finished replica, instead of a possibly erroneous original. But for this assignment, Amparo not only had the desire to write an original story. Confronted with the reality of "I don't know how," she had the *ganas* to want to know how, and her teacher — knowing what she was in for at the outset — nonetheless plunged in to help Amparo learn to create, not just carefully copy. The teacher saw, or more likely heard, Amparo's capacity to organize ideas, analyze and put together concepts, generalize, and compare. But she knew that something went "wrong" in the transmutation of these oral ideas into written words, since the result was incomprehensible "gibberish," and sentences sometimes required "translation." By undertaking Amparo's challenge, the teacher in fact became her collaborator: her response partner, her sense-maker, her sentence re-writer, her editor, her proofreader, and — I suspect — her title-writer.

The teacher took on the sole responsibility to "correct" and "translate" Amparo's thinking. This translation process might have begun with a two-minute, teacher-student conference to ask questions, react to content, and note murky areas of Amparo's first draft. It might also have involved abdicating some of this shaping power to fellow students. A sensitive and trained student response partner might help expand, extend, and clarify Amparo's thinking, and a skilled student editor (one with more skills than Amparo) might detect some errors in a preliminary proofreading. Giving Amparo the permission to work alone did not have to mean that she be deprived of the suggestions and corrective skills of her fellow writers. She might draft alone, but needn't write in a vacuum.

When the teacher confessed that twice she neglected to proofread overnight, I wondered how many proofreadings she did. One five-minute, teacher-student conference to edit the final draft — correcting spelling and sentence-level errors and re-writing portions — is enough, or if conferencing is an impossibility, one proofreading by the teacher. Since typing a clean copy was an issue, perhaps time and needless effort would have been saved if the teacher typed the final copy; the computer makes editing and correction so easy.

Was this extensive and intensive involvement worth it? Of course, yes! Amparo gained the prolonged and concentrated attention of her teacher, self esteem, pride of accomplishment, and recognition. But the teacher was plagued by her inability to correct students' composition problems and by the persistence of serious errors in Amparo's writing. This one success did not heal Amparo's mechanical wounds, and her errors will remain until she, not her teacher, learns to effectively amend them.

By commenting on this teacher's process and suggesting alternative strategies, I mean in no way to diminish her accomplishment and unflagging diligence. I just want to save a teacher's life, prevent a professional suicide. I realize once the commitment was made to Amparo, how difficult it would be to break promise with her yearning. The teacher's embrace of Amparo's need gave Amparo voice and gave her the opportunity to create and to know that . . .

> . . . when she sang, the sea Whatever self it had, became the self That was her song, for she was the maker.

> Wallace Stevens

EPILOGUE

Judith Shulman, Project Director
Far West Laboratory

This case was written in February. At the end of the school year, the author reviewed samples of Amparo's work and was surprised at what she found. The following excerpt is from a letter the author wrote to me:

> Here are some samples of Amparo's writing at the beginning of the year:
>
> ... look my Mother loves me but I now my litel broder is hers faborit and I dont come plane caus she listents to me and she cares enauf to sey none of us is her best in the other hand. ... (spelling, idioms)
>
> ... eventho I'am only fourteen years old the oraments and everything happens in a presentation[2] takes a hol year to find everything you wont but well doen. ... (syntax, spelling)
>
> ... my parents are very understandly and fare wen we need help for enything's my parents wont use to go strat to them my parents never have scrits between use even my Father has no choist but to tell wen somethings wong. ... (omissions, punctuation, spelling)
>
> When I wrote that piece on Amparo, there seemed to be no significant improvement in Amparo's writing, but really, now that I've reviewed her year's work, I see her editing skills have improved significantly (*when* I can *make* her proofread). Her routine spelling-vocabulary exercises now look great, although there are still many misusages with new items. Weekly spelling test scores for this semester range from 30 percent to 90 percent, with an overall average of 50 percent. Sentence boundaries are still a problem. There are a few paragraph indentations, a few transition phrases and overall improvements in idiom usage.

---

[2] A "presentation" is an anglicized word for "quinceañera" — a girl's 15th birthday party — considered to be a "rite of passage" in Mexico and other Latin American countries.

Moments of Truth: Teaching Pygmalion

"So, Ms. _____, how does it feel to be a minority? !"

These were the first words of the first student to speak to me in my first high school English class, remedial "contemporary" literature (for juniors). I stood in front of my new students, blue eyes staring blankly, realizing the accuracy of the question posed, and feeling at a loss for words (not a good sign for a "teacher of English"). I replied as honestly as I could, "I hadn't noticed. People are people to me, and I look at them for who they are, not what color they are."

The student, who loomed (he was 6'3") two feet from my desk (which I was leaning against for moral support), smiled and then quietly took his seat. The other students seemed to relax a bit, and I could feel some color returning to my pale face. And so, I passed my first test in urban education and learned an important lesson on interacting with my students: honesty, directness, and open sharing.

Being caught completely off-guard enabled me to get through that first "encounter." I didn't have a chance to think or react. I simply responded from my guts. But I later thought many times about that experience. I had grown up in a rural farming community, where my interactions with minorities had been limited to migrant farm workers who rotated in and out with the growing seasons. For the most part, I had scant experience with other cultures. I had been raised to be open-minded and accepting of other people. But it wasn't until I began teaching — first in a copper mining town where the predominant population was Hispanic, and now in the black community where my school is — that I discovered my true beliefs.

My school has the highest percentage of fights and personal assaults in the state. The students at this inner-city high school have characteristics common to other students in similar urban settings. Economically, they are at the poverty level; many are teenage parents; over 85 percent are nonwhite; the dropout rate hovers some-where around 18 percent; and absenteeism historically soars as high as 30+ percent. As far as I have been able to determine, the backgrounds of these students point to problems in their home environments, where parental supervision and support is almost nonexistent. Many are floundering and left to persevere as best they can — alone. However, "urban" or not, "deficient" or not, they were kids in *my* classroom and I believed *I* could make a difference.

I still believe that, but I'm also amazed that the trials and tribulations of dealing with urban students never seems to end. Early on, I had to confront my own issues about being a white teacher in a predominantly black school. I experienced my first pang of racism my second year here when I went to hug one of my black students who was sobbing over a personal conflict with a friend. For all my "openness" and "acceptance," I felt myself hesitate. It was only for a second, but that second haunted me for weeks. I asked myself over and over, "Am I a bigot? Am I prejudiced? " The answer came back, "Yes." Once I confronted my doubts and fears, however, I was able to make a change.

Still, six years later, I continue facing challenges related to race and socio-economic status. The outstanding challenge this year has been teaching George Bernard Shaw's *Pygmalion*. The play reflects some of Shaw's efforts at simplifying English usage — principally his omission of apostrophes in contractions such as *Ive* and *dont*. It also focuses on social equality and the relationship between what people seem to be and what they really are. Although these issues are as relevant today as they were in 1912, I was anxious about teaching this play to my students, whose social status is not always equal and whose perceptions of appearances are often jaded. I struggled with questions of how to present the material so that it would make sense to them and at the same time not be offensive.

In general, I feel most anxious when I have to teach literature units imposed by the district curriculum guide. Prior to the actual teaching of *Pygmalion*, I felt it was clearly an inappropriate selection because my students are both too removed from the themes of the story and too closely related to some of the characters. My dilemma became, "How do I bridge these opposing conflicts? " As the time to teach *Pygmalion* drew near, I noticed my palms sweating more often. It was harder to get out of bed in the morning. I knew that the key ideas, particularly the one about social equality, were sure to create a stir. In addition to my concerns about content, I worried about my students' language skills. Inevitably, literature units are difficult for my students to wade through, and the language manipulations in *Pygmalion* pose a particularly formidable task. How would I get them to understand Shaw's usage when they didn't comfortably grasp everyday usage?

I decided that if I had to follow the curriculum guide, I might as well use the strategies it provided for teaching the unit. Using the guide's key ideas as a base, I broke the play down into sections and matched them to pieces of the film, *My Fair Lady*. Once I had identified my primary objectives, I felt better. I decided to have the students focus on three key ideas: social equality, appearances, and personal identity. By emphasizing how the characters were defined through the manipulation of Shaw's language, I hoped I could keep the context impersonal.

To alleviate the boredom and resentment that inevitably coincides with inappropriate materials, my game plan was to have my students read the play aloud, answer discussion questions, develop and respond to their own essay questions, watch the film, *My Fair Lady*, as it paralleled each act (or section), and discuss the transformation of a play into a film. As the reading progressed, I would periodically interrupt to ask, "What is happening right now? Where are these characters? How do you know? What evidence supports your perceptions?" As pieces of the film were shown, paralleling the text, I would ask, "How is this section different and/or the

same as the text? What qualities does the film add to the text? How? What does music do for the text? For the audience? How is the audience affected by reading the text? By watching the film?" Finally, I would have students write answers (and then share their responses with the rest of the class) to another group of questions. Is proper speech still as important as it seems to Liza in *Pygmalion*? Why do you think people often base their impressions of others on the way they speak? What are the major conflicts in *Pygmalion*? How are these various conflicts resolved? Describe the various changes that occur in Liza over the course of the play. Describe the social setting of the play, particularly the contrast between the upper and lower classes. According to *Pygmalion*, what is the relationship between language and class? Between the way a person speaks and his or her identity? Why would aspects of appearance such as clothes, manners, and speech have such a profound effect on someone's life? What does *Pygmalion* suggest about the relationship between appearance and reality? What is the total effect of the play?

A week before I was to begin the unit, everything looked good. I felt ready and had things in place, but still I found myself restless at night and listless in the morning. In my eight years of teaching at an inner-city high school I have learned one absolute: no matter how thorough and organized you are, something unexpected will happen.

The first act — especially the part of Liza, the flower girl — was difficult and frustrating for my students. An excerpt of Liza's speech (with standard English comparisons) that gave my students particular trouble was, "Ow (Oh), eez (he's) y -ooa san (your son), is e (he)? Wal (Well), fewd (if you'd) dan y' de -ooty (done your duty) bawmz (by him as) a mather (mother) should, eed now (he'd know) bettern (better than) to spawl (spoil) a pore gel's (poor girl's) flahrzn than (flowers and then) ran awy (run away) athaht pyin (without paying)." After several pages I sensed their "I'm gonna quit this"

attitude intensifying. I stopped the reading and conducted my first discussion, focusing on Shaw's usage
and character development.

Me:	What kind of person is Eliza?
Students:	She's a bag lady!
Me:	Okay. Do you know people like her in your neighborhood? Have you seen people like her? [Heads nodded.] Would you agree with the description of Eliza as being like these people *you* see everyday, where you live?
Ryan:	She's like that fool on the corner next to the Burger King! [laughter]
John:	Yeah. Or that old cootie lady who pushes that ratty old wagon around. Man, you seen her hair with all them bugs crawlin' 'round it! [groans from other students]
Miguel:	Kinda like Martin, that druggie who's always begging for a handout or trying to touch you if you get too close.
Me:	All right. Now, which characters are the easiest for you to read?
Students:	Freddy and his mother and sister.
Me:	Who are you having the most trouble with?
Students:	That flower girl!
Me:	Why?
Students:	Because she's stupid!
Me:	Why do you think Shaw writes this way, for this character? What's his purpose?
Teresa:	To show she's ignorant.
Me:	Can you describe the differences between the way Freddy's mother and Eliza speak?
Chris:	Yeah. His mother knows how to talk.

[The discussion continued with me pointing out Shaw's
deliberate manipulation of language to further develop
and emphasize the characters of the play.]

As we resumed the oral reading, my students seemed
more relaxed and less concerned about struggling
through Shaw's usage. They'd had an opportunity to
vent their frustrations and understood that part of
Shaw's purpose was to get their attention. So that they
would better understand the content and characters, I
showed the first 15 minutes of *My Fair Lady*. This clearly
helped them hurdle Shaw's usage. They "got it" and
were willing to persevere.

Act II, and everything was going smoothly — or so I
thought. Again I asked my students to "think of the
people in your neighborhood who resemble Eliza." This
time the response came from a student who I knew was
involved in a gang, and could be dangerous if provoked.
"Ms.___ , why do you keep talking about *my* neighborhood? Why don't you talk about *yours*?" Inadvertently, I
realized, my remarks had been derogatory. Now the
gauntlet had been thrown at my feet.

I felt panicked and disappointed in myself. I knew I had
to respond quickly and carefully. "Let's stop for a
moment and discuss this. Jimmy has asked an important
question." I got up from the student desk I'd been sitting
in and addressed the class from the front of the room.
"I feel as though I need to tell you why I do some of the
things I do. Whenever I ask you to think of where you live
and people you know and things you've done in your life,
my intent is not to imply anything negative about you or
your lives or your neighborhood, but simply to have you
use what you already know to learn something new."
"Oh, okay," replied Jimmy. "Why don't you say 'downtown,' Ms.___? " offered Mark, also a gang member.

Something quite wonderful was happening: my students
were openly expressing their concerns, listening to
reason, and coming up with win-win solutions. They

were keeping my purposes and instructional strategies intact as well as their own integrity and self-esteem. "That's a perfect alternative, Mark. You've all been downtown many times and are familiar with the variety of street people there. With many prominent business and professional people downtown, you also see the extreme differences in 'social positions' in our city — like those represented in *Pygmalion*."

I had just wanted to smooth things over so we could get on with the lesson, but the outcome far exceeded my hopes. It seemed important to let the students know that they had helped me learn something. "I don't know how many of you realize what's happened here in the last few minutes, but it's very exciting," I said. "Thank you, Jimmy, for asking your question — it was appropriate and honest. You see, if you don't ask people what they mean when they say something, then you have to assume you know and that can create problems. Because you asked me to clarify and explain my statements in reference to where you live, we were all able to get involved and come up with a much better alternative. As far as I'm concerned, this is what a true learning process is all about — we all get something out of the experience."

The last thing I did was touch Jimmy on the arm as he left and once again thanked him for asking me to clarify my statements. From that day on, Jimmy made far more effort to contribute in a positive way and understand each lesson. He even arranged to take the final exam during his lunch hour because he wouldn't be in class on the day of the test. I can't say his life turned around, but he turned around in my class, and that's all I ask.

What I had learned about my students as people was that they couldn't differentiate between what they were reading, my references to their home lives, and themselves. In an effort to enhance the learning process, I had only succeeded in creating a situation of negative transfer. This had actually inhibited their ability to understand the literature because they were running on total emotionalism. My upper middle class white students never had trouble differentiating between themselves and a character like Eliza because the differences were so obvious. My urban students, however, were too close to Eliza. They related on an emotional level, as though I was talking about them in an unfavorable light. I was adding to their sense of hopelessness instead of helping them learn.

I made a few *faux pas* this year, and I know when I teach *Pygmalion* next year I will face some new challenges, but I'll also have some new resources. I will remember to distance my students from personally identifying with the characters of Eliza and her father. There are too many similarities and it creates confusion. My students feel *they* are being put down which makes an already difficult piece of literature almost impossible to comprehend. Probably the most effective change I made this year was incorporating parts of the film as my students read each act. I will continue to organize the teaching of this play in this way. Another especially helpful strategy for teaching this unit was limiting the number of key ideas. Focus is important with a text as rich in themes as *Pygmalion*. I would, however, like to add more current examples of these same issues. I think my students could benefit from associating with social issues that directly affect them and are central themes in the play (i. e., social equality). Perhaps what enables me to teach with such adaptability and relevance is the classroom environment that I develop throughout the year starting with day one. I have always fostered an atmosphere of openness and honest communication with my students (even when that *communication* seemed more *confrontation*), because I recognize my students' need to have a voice and be heard. Besides, I am the adult and have learned to separate my self from my behaviors. They, on the other hand, are still in the throes of learning this very complicated sense of objectivity.

Year after year I've relied on honesty, directness, and open sharing from my guts. I've found that when I am willing to learn, I am a model for my students, and then they are willing to learn. For me, that is education regardless of the setting.

Gloria Ladson-Billings
University of Wisconsin

This case is filled with important issues to be considered when dealing with diversity. However, in at least two instances, the teacher misses some key opportunities to develop a meaningful teaching-learning relationship with her students and to use the reality of their lives as a bridge to school-based learning.

Two aspects of the teacher's understanding of her students and the teaching situation are manifested in her willingness to be self-reflective. She was honest enough to question her own perceptions and prejudices when she hesitated before comforting the sobbing black student. The teacher was cognizant of that moment's hesitation in the same way black and other minority youngsters are cognizant of their minority status when encountering some slight or put-down, real or imagined. Always lurking in the back of one's mind is the question, "Did that happen because I'm black (or other minority)?" The question becomes the filter through which people sift their existence. The teacher confessed to this hesitation and examined it in a way that helped her better understand her own beliefs and attitudes toward her black students.

The second demonstration of this teacher's understanding came during her dilemma over the mandated reading selection. She was genuinely concerned about the appropriateness of the selection, *Pygmalion*, for her students. Her decision to focus on the ideas of social equality, appearances, and social identity provided her with relevant avenues through which to approach the material and engage the students.

Despite the teacher's fine efforts, I think her first missed opportunity came at the beginning of her case. She talked about the student who questioned her about being a "minority." Her response about not noticing color might have reflected her honest feelings, but it did not get at what the student was really asking. The

student wanted the teacher to know how he felt. Did she feel the same fear and trepidation that he sometimes felt? Did she feel the need to prove herself? Did she assume the blame and shame for transgressions of other members of her group? Although the teacher's response "satisfied" the students and got her "off the hook," she failed to realize that the question was not really about her. It was about her students.

The second missed opportunity occurred during the reading of *Pygmalion* when the student said, "... why do you keep talking about my neighborhood? Why don't you talk about *yours*?" The teacher does an excellent job recognizing that throughout the unit she has been alienating the students by making derogatory remarks about their neighborhood. However, her adjustment (shifting the discussion to people downtown) does not answer the student's fundamental question — "What about *yours*?" Although she has chosen the theme of social inequality, she did not choose to address the social inequality with which her students are confronted on a daily basis — the distance between their lives and hers. Even her choice to examine the situation of the people downtown failed to engage the students in the deeper questions about why and how these disparities exist in a land of plenty.

The teacher did use this teaching opportunity as a way to improve the relationship between herself and the students. She got to know them better as individuals with opinions and feelings. Perhaps the most common classroom experience of black students (and other students of color) is that of anonymity. They are unknown and unnamed in the classroom. Thus, her efforts to acknowledge the personhood of the students, no matter how small, is an important first step.

Somewhat tangential but equally important to this case is this teacher's perception that her students "didn't comfortably grasp the functions of [language] usage ..." To the millions of bi-dialectic speakers of black English and standard English, this statement would be funny if it were not so sad. If there is one skill that most black youngsters master early, it is language usage. It is central in their homes, churches and communities. The youngsters become "wordmasters" as they engage in the verbal repartee of "playing the dozens," "capping" or "toasting," and the hard-hitting social commentary of rap. It may be true that the teacher's students struggled with standard English and, yes, they certainly need to learn it. But, she needs to learn more about the language that students bring with them to the classroom.

Karen Desser, Teacher
San Mateo Union High School District

This teacher strives to bring an atmosphere of mutual trust and respect to her classroom. She wants her students to succeed in learning and to feel that she respects them as people, yet she needs to adopt additional strategies so that she can make further headway toward these goals.

I find it particularly fitting, if not ironic, that the teacher is leading her students through Shaw's *Pygmalion*. She is concerned that her students may have trouble in working with the language and syntax of the play, and no doubt this concern is justified, as descriptions of introducing students to the play's opening would suggest. Language is one of the most important issues presented in the play, which I will discuss below. But the teacher misses the opportunity for exploring Shaw's message about the underlying power and role of language. When I teach *Pygmalion*, I especially try to emphasize this message: acceptance by the dominant culture means recognizing its prejudices and learning to play along according to its norms. It often means that along the way you must suppress your own identity.

The play shows us Eliza's transformation from the underclass to the upperclass. It seems to me that this issue of cultural dominance is a key issue in the lives of the teacher's students. Indeed, they try to appraise her of this when they tell her that they feel she is maligning their community. Just as Shaw's Eliza is forced to choose between her own norms and those of the wealthy society Higgins represents, the teacher's students are confronted with a similar dichotomy.

The teacher is concerned about this dichotomy. But her students don't get the feeling that she is aware of their community's strengths. To them, it sounds as though she only knows about its problems. Her students try to point this out to her, but I don't think she understands.

By employing some different instructional techniques for teaching issues in *Pygmalion*, the teacher can better promote a classroom atmosphere of respect, trust, and success. The play presents two particular issues she could explore with her students that would allow them to identify similar examples in their own lives, in their community, and in contemporary society. The first issue is the role and power of language; the second issue is cultural dominance and assimilation.

In a dialogue presented in this teacher's narrative, she recounts the following exchange:

> Teacher: Can you describe the difference between the way Freddy's mother and Eliza speak?
>
> Chris: Yeah. His mother knows how to talk.

Chris's reply shows us many things, some of which should concern us all. He is all too aware of the discrimination involved with language. Eliza obviously knows how to talk too, but what Chris is pointing out is his first-hand knowledge that language equals power. Many educators have published articles presenting a variety of theories and suggestions on this subject, most notably Lisa D. Delpit, Judith P. Nembhard, and Geneva Smitherman. Given the teacher's concern for her students, I'm sure she would find these articles provocative reading. The articles could also be presented to the students and compared with the attitude toward language presented in the play.

Next, the teacher could have the students share their own views on these subjects. An ideal approach might be to generate student writing based on their own experiences with these issues. Students could interview each other and people in the community about situations they have experienced where language or language discrimination played a role. In this way, the teacher will learn more about the richness of her students' community and lives, and the students will have an opportunity to see how their experiences might parallel those of characters in literature they study.

On the issues of cultural dominance and assimilation, *My Fair Lady* portrays Eliza changing everything about herself in order to be accepted by Higgins and "society." The message is clear: you have to assimilate in order to "make it." Do this teacher's students agree? Does she agree? Since the teacher wants her students to explore the play's portrayals of class and power, she might develop an assignment where students investigate careers or goals that they aspire to. They could be given the task of interviewing someone who had attained such a career or goal, preferably someone from the racial, ethnic or social background that the student identifies with. Did that person feel the need to change anything about his or her heritage or personal sense of culture in order to succeed? Students can then compare the experience of their subject to Eliza's experience. Sharing the recently published *I Dream a World*, a photographic biography of 100 African-American women leaders, would be sure to spark student interest and inspire some creative investigations.

As the teacher recounts her thoughts before teaching *Pygmalion*, she says she "was anxious about teaching this play to my students, whose social status is not always equal." She feared the material would be "offensive" since her students were "too closely related to some of the characters." Her insights here are painfully accurate. But it is also possible to present the play from the perspective that Shaw's intent is to be offensive. He tries to incite his readers to examine the prejudice in the play, and examine their own society for such prejudice. Unfortunately, there are all too many parallels between this teacher's students and Eliza. What she can help them do is recognize, analyze, and work to eradicate such prejudice.

REFERENCES

Delpit, Lisa D. The silenced dialogue: Power and pedagogy in educating other people's children. *Harvard Educational Review*, Vol. 58, No. 3, 1988.

Lanker, Brian. *I dream a world: Portraits of black women who changed America*. New York, 1989.

Nembhard, Judith P. A perspective on teaching black dialect speaking students to write Standard English. *Journal of Negro Education*, Vol. 52, No. 1, 1983.

Smitherman, Geneva. Talkin' and testifyin' about black dialect: Past, present, and future tense. Adapted from "Soul 'n Style," a column appearing in *English Journal*, February, March, April, May, 1971.

Case 3

Attempting to Teach Self-Esteem

Teaching fills me with a nagging mix of joy and frustration. I devote my time, my thoughts, my dreams even, to the job, trying to do the best I can for people who deserve a job well done: the children in my second grade class.

A recent visitor commented that my class, more than any other she had observed, was a "real city class, so San Francisco." Ethnically, a third of my students are black, a third Asian, and the other third a mix of Spanish-speaking, Pacific Islander, and "other white." Economically, most of the students are from single-parent, low income families, and many live in the projects. Socially, my class reflects the struggles of young, mostly immigrant families, trying to survive in today's big city. Many have children for parents and consequently have been reared by their grandparents.

My students from such disadvantaged homes bear heavy burdens. Unrelenting poverty makes them believe that they are unworthy of the good things in life. To me it seems that these children have begun life behind others; they start with a negative score. It isn't fair, but in only two years of teaching, I have been hardened to think that it's unrealistic to expect it to change. At the same time, I can't help but believe I can make a difference. I am a city kid myself and a daughter of Asian immigrants. I never had it as tough as most of my students, but I do know what they go through. I see it every day in their faces, hear it in their voices, and feel it in their need for hugs. I want to convince these children that they are worthy. So I offered a lesson that I considered a lesson in life.

First I put a small hand-held mirror in a box. Then I had my students sit in a circle, and I presented the box, telling them that in it was a picture of "a very important person." I asked them to try to think of who that person might be. The children did not for one second think of themselves or their peers. They named adults, famous or influential in their lives, such as Martin Luther King, Jr., George Bush, their parents, their grandparents, their principal, even their teacher. We tossed their guesses around, then went on to discuss characteristics of the important person.

The concept of important characteristics, so abstract and slippery, was very difficult for the kids to understand. Ideas were sparse and faces blank, but I kept going. What is an important person like? What does an important person do? I kept prodding, but it was like pulling teeth. Finally, phrases such as "helps people," "loves others," and "is smart" came out. I wrote them on the board.

At last I chose Nathan to come up for a peek. Nathan, I knew, was the oldest of four boys from a modest home. He was a non-reader at age eight and a very sensitive boy who could cry simply because a peer told him that his (correct) homework was wrong. When Nathan peeked, I asked if he recognized the person. "Yes," he said, and I asked him to keep it a secret. He sat down and broke into laughter, hand over mouth, face red. The other children were dying to know who it could be.

Another student got up and took a peek. Her face lit up as Nathan's had. Yes, she knew this person in the picture. She giggled. The students were now very interested and curious.

After a fair number of children came up to look, I showed the whole class the "picture," putting it close to each face and asking if they knew who it was. No longer muddled and disinterested, their faces were alive and aware. I posed a question:

"What am I trying to say? "

Certain that my message was branded in their little heads, I expected overwhelming response. Much to my surprise, few hands went up.

"Alex, what am I trying to say? "

"That the picture is a mirror?"

"Neal, what am I trying to say?"

"That we are all people?"

"What kind of people?" I ask, pointing at the word on the board.

"Important people?"

"YES!" I exclaim. "We are all important people. Big or small, fat or thin, girl or boy. And we need to remember that every time we feel sad or lonely."

The faces were again going blank. I decided to stop and line the children up for recess. We'd be a little early, but it seemed we all needed the fresh air. I felt ready to cry. They didn't get it.

For many days thereafter, I discussed the lesson with my principal and my peers, going over my objectives, my technique, my approach, retracing the thoughts that had prompted me to do this lesson, to try to teach this concept. I blamed my lack of success on many things: those who spoke English only as a second language simply might not have understood; children from tough families in the projects might not be accustomed to praise.

I was sick of seeing students with low self-esteem, and I wanted so badly to do something about it. I chose the most direct way I could think of and needed to see results immediately. I remember feeling so disappointed, so much like things were out of my control. I wondered if I could make a difference. Over the course of the year, I can only hope I was able to convince them, if even for a fleeting moment, that they are somebody special. Some may never get it.

But I finally saw that some did. Denise, a quiet, unassuming little girl, wrote one day in her journal: "When I look in the mirror, I see a girl *who is important*." All the agonizing seemed suddenly worthwhile.

Since then I've tried this lesson again, with similar results. The one difference was that I was more prepared for my students' reactions the second time around. Telling a child that he or she is important may seem facetious to some. But I feel that they must actually hear it and know that at least one person in their lives believed it honestly.

I plan to keep doing this lesson every year. While I realize that one cannot convince another of his importance in a single hour, I will at least plant the seed.

*Peg Foley Reynolds, Teacher
San Francisco Unified School District*

In reading over this teacher's case study, my first thought was to wonder about the English proficiency of the children she teaches. My class is largely non- and limited English speaking. I often experience the resistance to discussion and the blank looks that she encountered. I have come to recognize it as a signal that I haven't given the children enough background to make the lesson meaningful.

I also have been trying very hard to raise the children's self-esteem. On the first day of school I had the class start a "My Me Book." Weekly we add a page or two to this book. In the book we tell all about ourselves, our families, our home, our pets, our friends, our likes and dislikes, etc. We make illustrations and share our pages with each other. We have discussions about how we are all alike in many ways, and different in just as many ways. At the same time we start an "opinions" book in which we tell what we think about things. I stress to the children that there is no "right" or "wrong" answer; they are just to tell what their thoughts and feelings are about different subjects.

I would like to try this teacher's idea of using the mirror hidden in the box after we had worked on the above two ideas for a number of weeks. Perhaps after being made to feel important by these class projects, they would be more open to a lively discussion!

*Amalia Mesa-Bains, Educational Scholar/Staff Developer
Far West Laboratory*

This lesson presents us with a learning situation in which something has gone wrong. Having recognized the tremendous stress experienced by her inner-city students, the teacher searches out a lesson that will lift their sense of self-worth. Her desire to convince them of their self-worth is a strong starting point. But the teacher knows that in discussing the concept of importance, she is in abstract and slippery territory. Her lesson involved a hands-on experience with a mirror and self-discovery, yet somehow even this concrete activity didn't work. What went astray in her lesson for improved self-image?

The instructor is on the right track when realizing that the lesson is based on a capacity too abstract. What is not working is the developmental readiness of her students to understand the abstractions so integral to the lesson. When the children respond to her questioning with names of famous and influential adults, it is the first clue to the failure of the lesson.

As youngsters whose identity is only partially formed, they are unable to perceive themselves as having the power that adults have to make decisions alone. They do not see themselves as separate and free from the powerful adults around them. Consequently, a lesson that emphasized the perception of "importance" instead of experiencing "importance" was ultimately ineffectual for these students. In this stage of their development the experience of competency, independence, and industry would ultimately contribute more to their sense of self-worth. When working with young people, we must always consider age-appropriate developmental tasks in planning learning activities. The life lesson was perhaps a greater lesson for the teacher about the importance of stages of growth and the very specific identity needs of youngsters that ultimately creates self-worth.

CHAPTER 2

Integrating Non-English Speakers into the Classroom

Because the number of limited English proficient (LEP) students has increased dramatically, many urban districts are struggling to find appropriate techniques to support them. Most districts offer bilingual programs to help students develop English skills, but these programs are limited and vary widely. Meanwhile, increased numbers of LEP students are being placed in regular classrooms with little or no support for the teachers. English-as-a-Second-Language (ESL) preparation and training for regular teachers ranges from good to non-existent. Our cases reflect this range of expertise.

In **Then and Now: Insights Gained for Helping Children Learn English** a teacher compares her early-career attempt to teach a non-English speaker with a similar situation 25 years later. She shares insights gained since the first experience, which had left her with a painful sense of failure.

Please, Not Another ESL Student takes place in a very different setting — the classroom of a teacher trained for bilingual education. The interventions, the students' role, and the instructional approaches portrayed in this case add to our understanding of the unique interplay between language and culture. We are able to see how effective new ESL support strategies can be.

Integrating non-English and LEP speakers into the classroom is one of the major challenges facing public education today. These cases reveal day-to-day issues teachers deal with as they try to address their students' linguistic and cultural needs. Along with the commentaries, they raise intriguing discussion questions about the role of the teacher, the significance of classmates, and the value of instructional models.

Case 4

Then and Now: Insights Gained for Helping Children Learn English

Last month a new student from Korea joined my third grade class. She spoke no English, and there was no one in my class nor in the school who spoke Korean. Yet she is learning English quickly, making friends, and is feeling comfortable in the classroom. In recent months, my class similarly welcomed a non-English speaking student from Chile and one from Russia. Again, no one in the class spoke Spanish nor Russian, yet these students are learning and feel involved. In fact, during my 25 years of teaching, I have often had students whose native language was not spoken by anyone else at the school. But all of these students learned English, made academic progress, and became actively involved with their classmates — except one. His name was Magnus.

It is painful for me to remember Magnus, a quiet, well-behaved 6th grader from Norway, who came to my class in my second year of teaching. Magnus taught me a great deal, but I didn't realize what I had learned until he was back in Norway. He arrived in February. His father was sent to the United States for six months on business and was able to bring the entire family. I met Mr. and Mrs. Nielson, Magnus, and his little brother Max, who was in kindergarten. The principal brought them all to my classroom about an hour after school had begun. I had little chance to talk with them, but the parents were friendly, fluent in English, and eager for their children to have the experience of an American public school and the opportunity to learn English. They left Magnus with me, and I gave him a seat. At that time I had 38 students, all seated in single rows. I remember introducing Magnus to the class, but I remember little more about that first day.

Each day I tried to work with Magnus. At that time there were no ESL classes, teacher aides, or classroom volunteers. I had no training and no experience working with limited English students, let alone non-English speakers. I would have him repeat phrases and do isolated vocabulary drills with pictures, and I spent a great deal of time pantomiming what I was trying to communicate. As the weeks went by, I found that Magnus was quite good in computational math. He was able to multiply and divide fractions and decimals and knew all about percents and ratios. But he was not learning English well at all. He participated in classroom activities as well as he could, but was not socially interactive. He had made no friends. Basically, he was isolated and ignored by his classmates. I saw his mother fairly often during the semester. I told her I didn't feel Magnus was progressing in English or making friends, but she said it was because he was shy. She felt he was happy and comfortable. In my heart I knew something was wrong, but I didn't know what it was.

During those months I saw little of Max, Magnus' little brother, because kindergarten was on a half-day schedule. One day in May I looked out my window and saw the kindergarten children playing in the school yard. There was Max, running and laughing and talking non-stop to his classmates. I couldn't believe my eyes. I went to his teacher at lunchtime and asked how he was doing. She told me how pleased she was with his progress. He had learned English so quickly and was able to communicate fluently with the other students. I felt miserable knowing how badly I had failed with Magnus. I didn't know what to do. I kept my failure inside of me and didn't talk to anyone. At the end of the semester, the Nielsons gave me a lovely gift, thanked me profusely for all I had done, and made me promise to visit them in Norway if ever I traveled to Europe. I felt so unworthy of their kind thoughts.

It took me a long while to figure out the problems. I believe I was so overwhelmed as a beginning teacher trying to sort out this multi-faceted job — curriculum, management, discipline, school politics, etc. — that I didn't have much time for self-reflection or for interaction with my colleagues. I never thought to ask the kindergarten teacher what she did or why she thought Magnus was not progressing as well as Max. It seemed that teachers never talked about their problems or revealed their inadequacies. In fact, it seemed that teachers interacted very little. Then one day I realized that interaction or lack of interaction was the key to the problem. I had never provided an environment where Magnus could interact with his classmates. The students were seated in straight rows and never communicated with each other except in the schoolyard. We had class discussions, oral reports, and questions, but they were teacher directed and non-interactive. I had taken the sole responsibility for Magnus' learning and never once had asked the other students to be part of the process or asked others in my profession for guidance. Max, on the other hand, had been in an interactive environment that focused on socialization and natural oral language development. In such a setting he learned easily and became an active participant.

When I think about Magnus now, I wonder what he remembers, if anything, about his one semester in an American school. My memories of those few months nearly 25 years ago, painful as they may be, have stayed with me and have made me a better teacher. Although I have learned much more about teaching students who are not native speakers, the most significant lesson I have learned is the danger of isolation and the importance of interaction.

SOME LESSONS LEARNED

When Sang Mi Pak arrived in my third grade classroom last March, she was accompanied by her father, her mother, her kindergarten brother, and an interpreter. The arrival of the family brought back the memory of the Nielson family entering my classroom so long ago. In fact, each time I receive a non-English speaking student my chest tightens a bit remembering my failure with Magnus.

The family had just arrived from Korea. Mr. Pak was able to understand a little English, but the other family members knew none. The interpreter introduced us and explained that Sang Mi had been given the "American" name, Sandy, in preparation for her entrance into American school. I explained that I would gladly call her by her Korean name, but he seemed somewhat insistent that she be called Sandy. The interpreter wanted to know if there were other Korean children in the class. I explained that there were two boys, both American-born and non-Korean speaking.

I may have learned some lessons, but I still had a long way to go. The day after Sandy arrived in my class, I had to attend a workshop and had a substitute. Sandy's father picked her up after school on her first day, so I explained to him what was happening. I asked him if he understood. He said yes, and thanked me for telling him. When I returned to school, I had a note in my box to call the interpreter. Mr. Pak thought I was leaving the class permanently and Sandy would have a new teacher for the rest of the school year. So much for understanding! I realized I needed to keep on-going contact with the interpreter for important messages. From that time on I talked with him almost every week. I also found a fifth grade Korean student, Sarah Kim, who was bilingual. I had her come into my classroom every morning at the start of school to see if Sandy needed to communicate with me. Sandy understood that she could call for Sarah at any time to help her. This arrangement was very effective, especially during those first few weeks.

My class is now arranged in tables of four, so I seated Sandy with three girls who were most eager to help her get adjusted. I explained to the class that each student has the responsibility to help a new student, especially one who does not speak English. It is their job to include and help direct the student in any and every school activity and to keep me informed of progress and/or problems that may arise. I realize that many of the things we do in the classroom are not comprehensible to a new student, but by inclusion — even if that only amounts to "going through the motions" — he or she does not feel quite so isolated and receives continual contact.

The school provides ESL instruction, but the instructor is part-time and was able to schedule Sandy only two days a week, for half-hour periods. Therefore, I rely on volunteers and the students to help me provide individualized instruction. Sandy is literate in her native language, so I was able to spend more time on oral language development and vocabulary. I have realized over the years that students need a period of time, often several months, to listen to a new language without being forced to give continual oral responses. In the beginning, I set up situations where Sandy responded with actions rather than words to various commands. This is called the Total Physical Response Method. When using it, I type up the commands from books I have collected or write my own. I give these commands to a student or a volunteer who says the command, models the action, and has the student perform the action with the volunteer and then alone as the volunteer states the command. The commands are usually in a series and involve useful vocabulary (e. g., washing your hands, sharpening your pencil, getting up in the morning, getting a glass of milk, etc.). These activities can be fun, and are non-threatening to the new student. I have found that as comprehension grows, speech spontaneously appears. I had different students work with Sandy each day so that she would get to know all the students and each student would feel responsible for her learning.

I provided Sandy with several simple workbooks (alphabet, beginning words, dot to dot, beginning English, etc.) that gave her things to do independently when no one could give her personalized attention. I often put her at the listening center with a book and tape, especially those books with an easy-to-understand story line and/or repetitive language patterns that would allow her to hear the rhythm and flow of English. It is hard to provide a quality language program within a regular classroom setting, but by fostering Sandy's natural oral language development and by providing her with continual opportunities for socialization, a great deal of language learning did occur.

Unfortunately, the school year ended just as Sandy was beginning to speak spontaneously. In fact, at our last-day-of-school barbecue, she asked me for a second hot dog. I was concerned that Sandy needed to be around English speakers during the summer to continue her progress. Through the interpreter I encouraged her family to enroll her in some kind of program such as summer school or childcare where she would be able to interact with other children.

I still have feelings of self-doubt about my ability to teach non-English speaking students. I probably always will, but I do know that my first painful experience with Magnus has made it better for Sandy and the many others who have passed through my classroom over the years.

*Alice A. Kawazoe, Staff Development & Curriculum Director
Oakland Unified School District*

"When I first came to this country, I was 10 years old and could speak only Chinese. The teacher put me in the back of the room and gave me an English book. He taught the class, but never again came to the back of the room, never gave me homework, never explained the classwork. I went through that first year at the back of the room, just listening, rarely talking to the other students or the teacher. It was a year of silence." Thus Maxine recalls her first year of American education 40 years ago, a year for her of learning by osmosis, despite the benign (or perhaps not so benign) neglect of her teacher.

I was reminded of Maxine's story as I read of this teacher's progression from the disquieting memory of Magnus 25 years ago to her most recent success story of Sang Mi or Sandy. Her two student stories constitute teaching snapshots in time, a kind of pedagogical "before" and "after." She did not relegate Magnus to the back of the room as Maxine's teacher did, but tried to steal bits of time "to work with Magnus each day," stressing repetition and vocabulary drills, and resorting to extensive pantomime. But she says she felt "miserable" and "unworthy" and like a "failure" when Magnus showed little progress after one semester in her straight-rowed class of 38.

Twenty-five years later, Sang Mi/Sandy entered into a totally different classroom. Clusters of students allowed for group talk and promoted students' sharing and learning from one another. Sandy's experience included listening centers, a fifth grade student-tutor-interpreter buddy, Total Physical Response, and — no small difference — a more knowledgeable teacher who was now comfortable with a wider repertoire of strategies to teach culturally and linguistically diverse students.

In many ways, this teacher 25 years ago was very much like Maxine, the new immigrant student. Each was isolated by space and circumstance, cut off from knowledge and assistance. How helpful just a few direct, uncomplicated suggestions might have been for both this teacher and Maxine. The teacher acknowledges that teachers "never talked about their problems" and, in fact," interacted very little." New teachers still generally get little more than a tour of the district, a pep talk by the principal, and a map of the school. Each year the P. E. coach, home economics teacher, or another errant soul without a full schedule gets cajoled, pushed, or blackmailed into teaching an English class or two. People get assigned to a grade level they've never taught or are confronted with student problems they do not know how to address. Veteran teachers may become so class- or subject- or department-bound that they insulate themselves from others and isolate their minds, building walls between classrooms that are more than physical. How may we tear down the walls that separate our students if we cannot or do not lower the barriers that cut off one teacher from another?

But the "before" and "after" snapshots of Magnus and Sandy give us hope. Twenty-five years later this teacher, still plagued by self-doubt, is a better and wiser teacher. Magnus, too, I am sure, learned something about himself in that semester of being a stranger in a strange land.

Forty years later, Maxine is a bilingual teacher, more skilled and sensitive than any she herself had. And one year later — because of her teacher and her classmates — Sandy is a learner, gaining confidence that will grow with each success, breaking her silence, and developing a voice that she will one day own. "Empowerment" is a fashionable word these days. This teacher empowered herself and thereby gave power to Sandy and all her other students. "Giving power to learners" — isn't that one definition of teaching?

Lois Meyer
San Francisco State University

The lessons learned during this teacher's 25 years of teaching are many and obvious when reading her comparison of "failure" with Magnus and "success" with Sang Mi. However, I would like to suggest a critically important lesson that may still remain to be learned: Be cautious about any such comparisons between second language learners. This caution hopefully may ease some of her pain about Magnus, but it may also cause her to question or qualify some of the lessons she feels she has learned about teaching learners such as Sang Mi. At least I hope it will lead this teacher to question, and thereby to probe even deeper.

Why does this teacher find herself comparing Magnus and Sang Mi? What makes them similar in her mind? They both entered her classroom as non-English speakers, that is true. But how comparable does that make these children? The teacher should ask herself: Why did each of their families come to the United States? Were they planning to make a new life here, or only to spend a brief time? Given these circumstances, why did each child want or need to learn English? Did they (or the parents) feel that learning English would be an interesting and fun challenge, or was it a crucial matter of survival and ultimate success for their life in this new country? Did the child himself or herself feel either of these feelings? Might one child simply have resented that the familiar language, school, and friends had been ripped away and now each day there was the frustration of a new language, new classmates, and a new reality to face? Or, since only English is spoken in the classroom, might another child desperately work to learn English in order to seem more like the other children, who see this newcomer as an ethnic and linguistic foreigner?

What about the presence of English at home? What are the differences between the two children in this regard, and what are the possible effects of these differences?

Which child might have received English support from the parents for lessons and homework, but might also have "hidden" shyly while the parents did the talking in English in social encounters at home and in the community? Which child might have had to struggle alone to learn English, or perhaps might have studied English along with the parents? But which child, at the same time, might be stretched linguistically by the need to use/practice English outside of school in order to translate for non-English speaking parents in the community?

This teacher's teaching strategies in the classroom were very different with Sang Mi than with Magnus. The single rows of seats have given way to tables of four where children are encouraged to talk with each other. Children are made responsible for each other's learning and well-being, and are asked to keep the teacher informed of progress and problems. They are entrusted with befriending newcomers and making them feel welcome. Each student is asked to take an active part as a volunteer language tutor in the TPR activities. When Sang Mi had to work alone, the teacher was prepared with a collection of independent materials and activities that nurtured her English skills at her own level of beginning proficiency. This teacher's sensitivities to the difficulties faced by second language learners in her classroom have increased tremendously across these years.

Very probably, Magnus would have appreciated the same support and active involvement in his learning that this teacher and her students provided Sang Mi, or at least some aspects of it. But again, some cautious questions must be asked: Do all children benefit from the same approaches to language teaching? Will the silent period be as long or as short, or will spontaneous verbalization be as rapid or as delayed, with all learners? Will all children respond to the opportunity or necessity to interact with their English-speaking classmates at tables or in volunteer tutoring situations? And, too, are all English-speaking children equally willing or sensitive when asked to interact with or to "teach" their non-English speaking peers? In terms of outcomes, did Sang Mi benefit in all ways more than Magnus? After several months of being removed from regular classroom lessons in order to spend most of her time in peer-led or independent language learning activities, she was beginning to speak spontaneously and to make requests (a second hot dog) in social situations (the school barbecue). Magnus, on the other hand, had spent some time with the teacher in language repetition and drill activities, but also participated as well as he could in the regular academic and social activities of the classroom. He seemed to interact little in class, but he was exposed to regular content instruction and was able to participate effectively enough in the math lessons to display his skills in computation. It seemed to the teacher that he was isolated and ignored by his classmates, yet his mother said he was shy, and she felt he was happy and comfortable. In the end, which child gained more in both language and academic development? Or was each one provided important opportunities for development which the other one lacked?

According to this teacher, Magnus' little brother Max seemed to succeed at acquiring English while Magnus failed, and she felt saddened and responsible for this comparison, too. But again, be careful about comparisons: Can 12-year-old Magnus be expected to learn English in the same way, or at the same pace, or with identical emotional response, as five-year-old Max? Does the excited playground chatter of a kindergartner present the same language challenge as the peer or teacher talk of a sixth grade classroom? Are Max's and Magnus' external circumstances in kindergarten and sixth grade, or their internal needs, fears, and motivations, so comparable that we can call one a "success" and the other a "failure" simply because their language acquisition histories were not identical?

To portray Magnus as a painful exception to the rule of successful second language acquisition is to assume that such a rule exists. In the process of second language acquisition in school, there are few firm rules. A considerable research literature, summarized by McLaughlin (1984), now documents the many differences that children display as they go about the task of acquiring a new language. Some of these differences, such as wholistic vs. analytic learning styles and strategies, or a child's gregarious vs. inhibited attitude toward social contacts with native speakers, are highly individual. Other differences seem to be influenced by the child's home culture, dominant language, or level of English language proficiency. For example, Wong-Fillmore et al. (1985) found that Chinese children, especially those with very limited English proficiency, tend to acquire English language skills best in relatively quiet classrooms where peer talk is reduced and contact with the teacher in structured language lessons is increased, since "they depend more on adults for input than they do on peers." On the other hand, these researchers found that Hispanic students tend to acquire these best in classrooms where talk with friends is encouraged, for "the more opportunities they find to use English with peers, the more they gain in production and comprehension." Despite these group tendencies, individual differences still show themselves. One Chinese child may thrive and acquire English through chatter with English-speaking friends while another remains silent; a quiet Hispanic child may be intimidated by the peer talk that motivates her classmates and instead gain skill and confidence through structured, teacher-guided language lessons.

Given all these questions, is the author really a "better" teacher now than she was 25 years ago? Despite my caution about comparisons, I would unhesitatingly say, "yes." In my opinion, this is not due to her teaching methodologies or classroom grouping practices, important though they may be. Rather, the teacher's true quality is seen in her keen sensitivity to Sang Mi's probable confusion and loneliness in the classroom and in her willingness to adapt her teaching and classroom climate in ways that make Sang Mi feel welcome and able to participate with confidence. Another second language learner might come into the classroom tomorrow needing a different kind of attention and responding to different teaching strategies. I feel certain that the teacher would bring this same sensitivity and caring concern to the task of trying to provide what this child needed and to adapting herself and her teaching, as much as possible, to this child's uniqueness.

REFERENCES

McLaughlin, B. (1984). Individual differences and language learning strategies. Chapter 5 of *Second language acquisition in childhood: Vol. 1 — Preschool children* (Second edition). Hillsdale, NJ: Lawrence Erlbaum Associates.

Wong-Fillmore, L., McLaughlin, B., Ammon, P., & Ammon, M. S. (1985). *Learning English through bilingual instruction*. Final report to the National Institute for Studies in Education. Berkeley, CA: University of California at Berkeley.

Case 5

Please, Not Another ESL Student

Sam Garcia, the Spanish bilingual counselor, stood outside my classroom door, grinning sheepishly as he pointed me out to the new student. I knew why they were at my door, and without really intending it, I stopped talking in mid-sentence and blurted out, "Oh, no, not another ESL student!" Glaring at Sam, I shook my head in despair and moaned, "You can't do this to my program."

He looked beyond me; his eyes refused to meet mine.

"See the boss."

"But I have! "

"You'd better go see him again. Rumor has it we're the only school that'll take in these kids the rest of the year."

"Damn," I muttered. I felt so powerless. The middle school I had chosen to teach in because of its diverse student population, its location near the heartbeat of the city, its array of special programs — Spanish bilingual, Chinese bilingual, reading demonstration, band, and home economics — was now testing my strength, my endurance, and my creativity.

Sam disappeared, and the dark eyes of my new student caught mine. The class watched us closely. "Bienvenido, Fernando, bienvenido a los estados unidos, a San Francisco, a nuestra clase."

Later, during my prep period, the last of the day, I was as usual too tired to do any "prepping." I looked down the list of names and dates in my rollbook. It was May 1st, and 20 new students, including Fernando, all zero-level English, had entered my classroom since February. My "program" had been sorely affected — not enough books, paper, chairs, tables, dictionaries. Even worse, not enough teacher time for students thrust so abruptly into a new language and culture. From my experience teaching in Central America, I knew that these students were arriving in this country after completing their

school year in December and then traveling during summer vacation to this new country, expecting to enter school in March or April to begin a new year. Unfamiliar with our September-June school year, they had no idea that school would soon be ending. Nevertheless, here they were, assigned to my combined 6th, 7th, and 8th grade Spanish bilingual classroom. And so far, the best I had been able to do was give each a hasty welcome, then move silently closer to hysteria over how I could make the transition work for everyone.

I knew I had to think of something quickly. The week before, 11-year-old Araceli didn't make it to the girl's bathroom in time; she hadn't been able to remember where it was and had been too shy to ask another student. The long corridors circle the building, and sometimes, on certain floors (who knows why) the bathrooms are locked. Araceli, embarrassed and frightened, went home. I, her new teacher, felt guilty, frustrated, and angry. We both needed help.

It was too late in the year for extra help in the classroom, but I thought of my colleague Carolyn, teaching in the basement, publishing poems and stories, putting on plays, and enjoying the fruits of her year-long emphasis on writing and creative learning. She taught the sixth grade honors class during the same two-hour block my Spanish bilingual students were with me for English-as-a-Second-Language and science instruction. I wondered . . . how about pairing up each ESL student in my class with a native speaker from her class?

We met and talked and agreed! Yes! And the planning began. How should we pair the students? We went over our class lists, noting problem students. I pointed out that many of the newly arrived Spanish-speaking girls would be most comfortable with a female partner because they come from Latino school systems that traditionally separate the girls from the boys. Carolyn mentioned that she had a number of Asian girls who also were accustomed to working with each other. We made as many pairs of girls as we could. After that, our pairing was based on an attitude of "let's try these two and see if it works out; if not, we'll change it."

In planning the substance of the partnership program, I thought of my original goals in initiating the contact with Carolyn: I wanted someone besides myself to befriend my bilingual students, and I wanted my students to feel important and wanted in their new country. My aim was to provide culturally relevant material in English and Spanish that would help them learn another language and make friends too.

I put together a packet of basic information that students expect to learn when they are studying a new language. The packet contained days of the week, months of the year, numbers, simple dialogues, the alphabet (for spelling purposes), weather words, a map of San Francisco with questions about addresses and phone numbers. I had spent a number of years teaching in Central and South America and knew that certain games such as Bingo ("loteria"), Simon Says ("Simón dice"), and Twenty Questions ("veinte preguntas") crossed cultural boundaries; therefore, I included them in the packet and also introduced simple crossword puzzles based on the new vocabulary they would acquire in each language.

The packet was prepared in both English and Spanish with a blank page for writing between each section, since we knew the students would want to practice writing their new vocabulary. Even though the material was available in both languages, I pointed out to Carolyn that it was important to keep instruction in each language as separate as possible so that students did not rely on back-to-back translation as a method of learning a new language. Therefore, we agreed that our Monday session would focus on the material in English and the Friday session would be held in Spanish. Back in our own classrooms we would have our students record their experiences and feelings about the partnership program in their journals in the language of their choice.

Carolyn and I will never forget the first partnership session. The initial meeting of partner with partner was heavy with apprehension. Some paired students couldn't even bear to look at each other out of nervousness, shyness, fear. We passed out a curriculum packet to each student, had the students write their names on the packet cover, and gave initial instructions. Silence. I thought I had made a big mistake. And then, as minutes passed, there began tentative talk. Within 10 minutes, Carolyn and I were able to grin at each other. As we looked around the room, we saw body language, sign language, drawing for communication. We heard laughter, words being repeated, introductions, and yells for help too! We saw and felt an intensity of learning that had an energy of its own. Kids were interacting with kids and their attention to each other was 100 percent!

Looking back, we felt more could have been done. We found that once the students began using the simple learning packet, they had many questions that could have been answered if they each had their own bilingual dictionary. We only had two globes, yet a student's natural curiosity led him or her to want a map of the world to find out where a partner's native country was located. Even the students born in the United States had often moved from state to state or city to city, so we needed maps of the United States to allow them to show and talk about their many homes. Once the English-speaking students had mastered the pronunciation of the Spanish alphabet, they were eager to try reading in Spanish, but we had too few books.

Beyond supplies for the program, we wondered about the curriculum itself for next year. How could we challenge the students? What about science? Could students work on experiments together? What about having the students work on major interdisciplinary projects that incorporate English language arts and science?

As a trained bilingual teacher, I knew the value of native language instruction. I knew that my most successful bilingual students were those who had received the most instruction in their native language. I agreed that whatever we decided to work on in our Monday and Friday sessions would have to be presented to the students in my own classroom in prior lessons in their native language. In that way we would be building on what students already knew and understood. In addition, this approach would help the students understand the material presented to them in a new language.

We wondered about ways to pair and group the students. Given the short amount of time we initially had to put the program together, we certainly had paid too little attention to the pairings. There had been some problems. Also, absences had caused problems. These situations led us to the following questions: Do the students always have to be in pairs? Maybe they could form cooperative groups of four. Do they have to stay with the same partner all year? Wouldn't it help stretch their experiences by matching them in a variety of ways throughout the year? As teachers, we might also observe the partners and learn from their behavior. Which kids were helpful? Why? Was it behavior that we could model so that those less helpful could improve? We were excited. We were onto something. We agreed to meet at the end of the summer to lay out next year's plan.

In June, a few days after school was over, I found Alonzo Jones' journal in Carolyn's classroom and read this entry:

> This is the first time I've heard that we will meet
> with the ESL class about teaching them English.
> For our field trip together I don't know what it
> will be like. But I believe that it will be fun.
> Somehow I will do what I can to communicate
> and help my partner.

It's comforting for me to know that I need not be alone with my ESL students, that I have Alonzo and many others like him to help me out. I had based my Spanish bilingual program on the premise that I, as the classroom teacher, was the only one who could work with Spanish-

speaking newcomers to our school. I now reali
mistake. Learning about a new language and
come not only from a teacher but from one's
speaking peers.

*Alice A. Kawazoe, Staff Development & Curriculum Director
Oakland Unified School District*

The pairing of students — in this case, ESL students with native speakers — is a simple but powerful practice. Encouraging students to talk with their peers promotes their oral skills and, perhaps more importantly, gives them a real audience and purpose for their thinking. To have someone who will listen is no small reward, and how fortunate for the speaker if the listener is as earnest and willing as Alonzo Jones who will ". . . do what I can to communicate and help my partner."

When teachers prepare or train students to work as partners, as these two teachers did, then students will 1) more freely talk or write about their life experiences, 2) clarify and elaborate on those experiences for their partner, 3) value their experiences, and 4) discover that they have stories to tell that someone would like to hear.

Talking with someone often liberates ideas from the confines of the mind. Students struggle with "getting ideas out," and they worry too much about what to say, how to say it, how to start, how to end, choosing the right word, spelling and punctuation, being correct — all part of a "cognitive overload"[3] that obstructs expression and communication.

The following classroom example illustrates clearly the power of peer partners and reaffirms the "intensity of learning" that these two teachers discovered when "kids were teaching kids."

ONE STUDENT'S WRITING PROCESS

In the crowded classroom, desks are pushed together in pairs, and the din of voices would rankle the sensibilities

[3]Hays, J.F. & Flower, L.S. (1980). The dynamics of composition: Making plans and juggling constraints. In L.W. Gregg & E. R. Steinberg (Eds), *Cognitive processes in writing*. Hillsdale, NJ: Lawrence Erlbaum Associates.

of any administrator who deems quiet busy work a cardinal virtue. Two young men sit, hunched over their desks — one tense with concentration, carefully and methodically reading the words; the other leaning slightly forward to hear, eyes focused on the page, following the reader's voice.

"Hey, is this stuff true?"

"Yes."

"Wow. . . ." Steve Meagher shakes his head in amazement, stretches out his legs, and leans his six-foot-four-inch frame back in his chair, looking every bit like the basketball player he is. "Tell me about the war and what it was like to fight."

Chiam Chitavang takes a deep breath. He has the body of a sixth grader with the face of a middle-aged man. "Well. . . it hard tell," he begins, slowly unraveling his war stories as a 14-year-old soldier in Cambodia. To escape the Khmer Rouge, Chiam and his brother fled into the hills and spent months foraging for food and dodging capture which meant sure death. He killed and saw his brother killed by a landmine. Chiam walked alone for four days to a refugee camp in Thailand, where, after eight months, he was miraculously reunited with his mother, sisters, and younger brother. "My life much struggle," he says.

"That's no lie," Steve says, "but what you need to do is to write down what you just told me 'cause what you said is really live, and what you wrote is kinda boring."

Thus begins that delicate art of response, that dialogue which leads to revision, to expansion, to elaboration, to showing in words. Each student in the ESL/Remedial Writing class is struggling to gain enough facility in writing to pass the school district's Writing Proficiency Test. Response partners in this class consist of one English speaker — albeit remedial or reluctant — and one newcomer to the language.

At our school, newcomers now come from 50 countries and speak 33 different languages, including Spanish, Cantonese, Mandarin, Korean, Vietnamese, Tagalog, Ilocan, Cambodian, Arabic, Hindi, Portuguese, Laotian, Hmong, Lao-Mien, Punjabi. How does one teach this class of many colors, this multicultural, crayola-box class?

We teachers quickly saw that we needed to slow down to give students the time to think and give ourselves time to get off our assignment treadmills and catch our breaths. We had been rushing headlong from assignment to finished product, leaving little room in the schedule for directed and useful pre-writing or re-thinking and re-shaping. This pace might result in more scores in the grade book, but it didn't lead to more writing proficiency.

Students needed more time and more individual help. They needed modeling to learn how to respond to their partner's writing; how to make suggestions; how to re-envision their writing and make it grow. So we teachers learned to elongate the writing process. We began to teach skills in the context of the student's own writing so that the students, in turn, could edit and proofread.

Rather than existing as compartments of isolated information — grammar in the workbooks, reading in the literature anthologies, pre-writing in the dittos, writing in the notebooks, journals in the folders, vocabulary in the dictionaries, creative writing in Never-Never Land, and scores in the gradebook — the components of our language arts instruction began gradually to fit in, make sense, synthesize into a meaningful whole — a process.

Nowhere is that process more evident than in the ESL/Remedial Writing class with writers like Steve and Chiam. Chiam's first draft of a memoir which he read aloud to Steve is a short and simple narrative:

> I know the war and what the war make on mankind. War put much strife. The job of soldier

is to shot and kill. It much easy to shot in a dark.

Steve, ever curious about war and violence and perhaps fascinated by the lethal experiences buried within the small body of his response partner, first invited, then coaxed Chiam to talk about the fighting and killing he had done. "Tell me more. . . I want to know more. . . ." Finally, after halting explanations, more questions, and more talk, Steve returned to Chiam's paragraph, under-lined the last sentence and asked him 1) to explain what he meant (Does he mean shooting into a dark place? Does he mean shooting at night? Why is it easy?), and 2) to write about a time, an incident, when it was "much easy to shot in a dark."

Here is Chiam's revision:

> I know what the war and what the war make on mankind. War put much strife. The job of soldier is to shot and kill. We the soldiers walked at night so not one can see us. Hot the air and all thing is quiet. We hear the ground sigh under our shoes and the bushes scratch us and break. One or two houses sit. "Out, get out," we yell again and one more time. No body come out. But from the houses noises heared, so we shotted fast.
>
> It much easy to shot in a dark. The bullets have not eyes to see the body it kill. The bullets have blindness. I have eyes to see but the dark is better to hide eyes. Why do I kill? Because it is war. War in a dark is much easy for the soldier to kill.

Chiam's essay will undergo one more step — the editing stage — but his revision has made a prodigious leap forward. Perhaps a better metaphor is Chiam's own: his essay is an explosion of ideas triggered by his partner, Steve, who by his directed and focused questions, fired Chiam's thinking. As Steve said earlier, "Wow" — to both of them.

CHAPTER 3

*Interactions
with Students*

Student-teacher interaction is an encounter of perceptions, values, and attitudes. A teacher's awareness of these elements, and understanding of where and how teacher and students may differ, can help that teacher develop positive relationships with each child. As educators, we have paid too little attention to how critical such personal relationships can be: they often set the stage for appropriate instruction and effective learning.

The narratives in this chapter focus on significant teacher-student interactions. These cases deal with questions of race and language, as well as issues of poverty, peer pressure, broken promises, abuse, and failures in the system. Settings range from inner-city to newcomer schools. Each teacher struggles to create learning and provide support. Yet, clashes of cultural values and expectations often bring frustration and conflict.

The first three cases describe teachers' interactions with African-American students. In **Fighting for Life in Third Period**, a returning teacher's naive expectations come up against the harsh realities of an inner-city school. A forthright account of cultural and racial interchange, this case elicited some of the book's most passionate commentary.

In **Drained by One Troubled Child: Did I Help?**, the teacher must handle the classic conflict between the demanding and sometimes unanswerable needs of a special student and fairness to the entire class.

The story of a boy named **Darius (I Hope He Makes It!)** is a touching reminder of our heroic attempts to keep faith with our students when everything in our educational system seems to work against those relationships.

The case is marked by traumas of family abuse, student anger, and a teacher's own sense of regret.

A Trip to Hell and **From "Outsider" to Active Learner: Struggles in a Newcomer School** show the linguistic and cultural needs of Latino students in two very different settings. **A Trip to Hell** brings to light the problems one teacher faced because of the school's student grouping, instructional practices, and dual languages, coupled with contradictory district expectations.

In contrast, **From "Outsider" to Active Learner** takes place in a monocultural Latino school with clear district expectations. But crises still erupt as the teacher tries to deal with dual cultures and establishes social supports and trust. By studying the teacher's pivotal role in these moments of crisis, we can begin to examine the larger concerns of our bilingual/bicultural education practices.

Case 6

Fighting for Life in Third Period

It was the first day of school — and the first day of my return to public high school teaching after 15 years of homemaking and public relations work for private schools. The first two classes had gone well. I felt confident that my teaching skills, though rusty, were "there" to recall and practice. The students had seemed responsive to my enthusiasm and had been friendly and cooperative.

The students, in fact, fascinated me. This high school comprised mainly minority students: 30 percent African-American, 55 percent Hispanic, and 15 percent white. Most of the families in this semi-rural area on the outskirts of this large metropolitan city are working class, but many are poor. Although special programs had overcome *de facto* segregation throughout the city, this high school was still largely segregated and had a reputation for campus disorder and low achievement. Now, the increased integration and improvement of this school was a top district priority. A major part of this new effort was to raise the teachers' expectations for student achievement and to hire more teachers so that in-class hours could be reduced. Teachers were expected to use much of their time outside of class for student and family contacts such as tutoring, phoning students' parents, and visiting their homes. I was one of these new teachers. I had jumped at the opportunity to work in a program that addressed the students' needs for more help. And I was especially interested in helping minority students prepare for a successful and responsible American life. I was tired of my own "white middle class" life and wanted to broaden my experience by working with other kinds of people. I felt we could learn from each other.

Nothing in the three-week orientation I'd been through, or the first two classes of the day, seemed to prepare me for what I was about to meet in third period. The students were much noisier coming in. When I launched into my idealistic speech about how they were the star players, the performers, and I was their coach, they laughed and someone called out, "Who's the quarter-

back? Where's the ball?" Whereas the first two classes had been quiet and attentive as I explained the special opportunities that lie ahead for qualified "minority" peoples in the decades to come (as American whites decrease in number while all minorities increase), this class seemed totally uninterested. The more I tried to explain the "new high school" — with genuine new expectations — the more restless they became. Someone mumbled that the old school was just fine.

Fifteen minutes into the hour, big trouble entered the room. Stout, black, stuffed into a flame-red dress, Veronica sauntered slowly, insolently past me and took a seat as conspicuously as possible. She grinned slyly and said in a loud, husky tone, "What are you, some kind of fake white preacher lady?" The class burst out laughing and three large black boys suddenly jumped out of their seats and began literally dancing around the room, spontaneously rapping about the situation, clapping their hands, calling out "Yea, Sister!" This was how I met Veronica, Travis, Lee, and "Larry Luv." Before long I had named them "The Gang of Four."

Gathering up my strength, I ordered them into their seats and quickly moved into the day's business: checking out textbooks and handing out Student Information cards on which they were to write their schedules, phone numbers, interests, activities, etc. When the hour passed finally, Veronica was the last to leave. Haughtily she flicked her card onto the desk. In a second-grade scrawl she had penned a very personal message to me: "I can see rite now you never going to make it as a techer. This class going to walk all over you." She was right. They did.

During those first nightmarish days, I felt I had run into the worst of everything I had heard about in the ghetto: crude, foul language, rudeness, low achievement, blatant sexuality, continual talk of violence, guns, drugs — the works. These students would have been a fearsome group in any color, but their blackness seemed at first to be a barrier. I was not sure what *really* to expect from them. Were they truly capable of decent behavior? Did they need some other kind of schooling?

What saved me from indicting *all* the black students was the obvious fact that in my first two classes I had wonderful students of all ethnic groups who defied these ghetto stereotypes, who were courteous, well-behaved, and capable. Their skills in speech and writing would certainly enable them to compete successfully for placement in a job or college. I was delighted to know and work with them.

What I gradually realized was that the antics of The Gang simply represented bad behavior — period. The cultural ways they expressed defiance of authority were only on the surface, where color is. Basically, success in school or anything else depends on certain attitudes that are universal. The high expectations the school held for its students were without regard to color. For the sake of The Gang, myself, and the rest of the class, I had to get control of the situation.

However, I could not seem to do this by myself. Because the students "fed" on each other, I quickly found that reprimanding any of them in front of the others only set everyone off. Veronica, especially, challenged me whenever I got after the boys; she also taunted me when I didn't! For Veronica, I could do nothing right.

So, behind the scenes, I desperately sought help from all the resources I could find: I called conferences with parents, counselors, and other teachers; I wrote discipline referrals to appropriate vice-principals and sent notes to the football coaches; I also invited our "resident" staff development expert to watch me teach and give me classroom management pointers. Three times I had to call the security force to have unruly students removed. I am deeply grateful to say that everyone gave me unquestioning support right when I needed it. Without their ready cooperation, I might not have made it.

With this extrinsic support, the class became somewhat manageable. I learned things about The Gang that gave me some sense of power. Veronica was taking the course for the second time. She had to pass it in order to graduate in January so she could take a job in a hospital and support her baby. I learned that Larry did care very much about what his family and fellow church members thought about his conduct in school. And I found out that Travis and Lee had no fathers, their mothers "couldn't do nothing with them," but that both boys had many times resisted the temptation to drop out of school. They were still "hanging in" and truly did want that English credit. They also did not want disciplinary referrals and did not like getting dragged out of class by Security. By talking with them privately, reminding them daily of their desire to pass English, and issuing threats (backed up by action) if they got seriously out of line, I achieved an uneasy peace.

Nevertheless, there was still a very serious problem. I now had a total dread, even hatred, for this class. It was as though I had suffered so much shock and rejection during my first weeks with them that, in spite of improvement in their behavior, my negative feelings about them remained. Every day I would happily conduct other classes — trying out techniques in student empowerment through cooperative learning —all the things I'd come there to do — except in third period. The minute those students walked in the door, even the ones who had never given me any trouble, I felt the old stomach-tightening nausea sweep over me.

One day as I looked into their faces, I saw that the misery I was feeling was mirrored in their eyes. The good students were powerless to do anything about all the trouble. And the Gang of Four seemed incapable of actually exerting positive leadership. I realized that I, myself, was the only person in that room who could solve the problem. *It was my responsibility!* Even though I hadn't deliberately started the trouble, it was my role to find a solution. I needed to be not just a teacher, but a true leader in solving a group problem.

After anguished soul-searching, I came up with the following plan: I began by talking honestly to the class. I told them I was miserable with them, and that I sensed they were miserable, too, but that we didn't have to be this way. I said I felt they must have some important things to teach me about teaching and that I was willing to learn from them. Then I asked them to form groups of three or four students and discuss the following questions with each other: 1) What kinds of activities make an English class a good one? 2) What are the responsibilities of a teacher toward the class? 3) How can the students help make the class a good one? Each group was to designate one student to write down their main ideas and report to the class as a whole after about 20 minutes of discussion.

I adopted this plan for several reasons. Though I felt my own wounded psyche wouldn't be able to stand a direct onslaught of criticism, I wanted everyone to be able to express negative feelings freely and anonymously. I also wanted to direct their thoughts (and mine) toward positive solutions for the future after the negative thoughts had been vented.

When it was time for the group representatives to give their reports, I sat in a student seat with the class, and listened carefully to what they wanted to teach me. The first section contained all the contradictions I had expected. They wanted more reading, less reading; more writing, less writing; more discussions, fewer discussions; and, of course, lots of field trips! Then with great sincerity and dignity, they explained the teacher's responsibility: "The teacher should take control of the class; the teacher should make up her mind about plans and stick to them; you shouldn't try too hard to please us. . . just be yourself; the kids should be more afraid of the teacher than she is of them; throw out the kids who make trouble. They shouldn't be here." Several looked

directly at me as they talked, and I was frankly impressed with their genuinely helpful attitude. Finally, they acknowledged that the responsibilities of the students were to come to class and cooperate. One boy remarked solemnly, "Not all of us have been doing this." There were embarrassed smiles.

When the end of the hour came and they had walked quietly out, I was left with tears in my eyes once again. Only this time they were not tears of humiliation, but of gratitude and humility. The students had called on me to take charge and do my job! They wanted what I wanted — an orderly room in which to do our work, a room where there is trust and productivity. If I didn't succeed, neither would they! Why did I need to hear this from them — something I should already have known? I'm not sure, but from that day on things became better. I had the courage to absolutely, unequivocally require decent behavior and language from anyone who wanted to stay in my class — period! I had no fear of demanding conformity to constructive standards of behavior regardless of racial or cultural differences. Knowing that I had the students' mandate to take complete control made me comfortable in doing this. I felt more relaxed and able to "be myself." Paradoxically, the more I felt I had power, the less I had to use it overtly. I began to like the students as individuals, and I felt they liked me. I could give the students choices, put them in structured work groups, let the noise level rise when I wanted it to — all because I knew that underneath there was teacher control at all times.

Toward the close of that semester, I knew Veronica would pass (much to her relief and mine) and that I would "pass" as a teacher, too. The crowning moment for us all came when I performed a rap I'd written myself, with the irrepressible Larry, Lee, and Travis swaying behind me, providing the back-up rhythms!

REFLECTIONS

Now that I have finished my second year at this school, I feel that my early problems were a combination of lack of recent experience in the classroom, lack of much experience with other races, and inexperience with the effects of poverty. All three of these are different issues. In a nutshell, I learned to depend on the following principles:

1) No matter what kind of students you have, **always** establish teacher control first. Everything else can follow. The students expect you to do this and won't respect you if you don't. They are not intimidated by reasonable control; they are reassured by it. Nobody wants to be in a confused situation. And be careful not to sound too idealistic. Students mistake altruism for weakness. Firm (but humane) discipline programs are needed in class *and throughout the school.*

2) Brown-eyed, dark-haired Hispanic and African-American students do not fear or resent white teachers; they are used to them! And, as you take these students into your life and heart, you yourself lose all sense of color. They become individuals to you — real people. For me, this constant contact with "other" kinds of people has been all that I was hoping for. I find that in the malls, on the streets, I hardly notice that people are "different," because in fact they actually don't look different to me. While we wish that there were more minority students going into the teaching field, and we are actively promoting this movement, I do feel that at least some white people (teachers like me) are getting a very good multicultural education by teaching in inner city schools. Also, I feel that many of these students will remember a kind and interesting white teacher or two who helped them. Surely this will promote a little more racial harmony in our country.

3) Race and poverty are not necessarily synonymous. Many of our African-American and Hispanic students come from good homes where there is fine support. These students are doing very well. Other students are achieving a great deal against tremendous odds. (One stereotype that was thoroughly smashed for me during the last two years was the idea that Spanish-speaking immigrants do not learn English. Well, the parents may not learn it, but the students do! One of the top-achieving boys in the freshman class was a student of mine whose parents don't speak any English.)

4) It is poverty that is the real enemy. This is too big a subject to tackle here, and too complex. What I strive to do every day is to help students get over what I call the "poverty mentality" — the apathy, laziness, hopelessness that will surely doom them to perpetual poverty if they can't see beyond it. Do we truly feel that an individual, by his or her own efforts, can succeed? Most of my students do feel they can, and so do I.

Gloria Ladson-Billings
University of Wisconsin

This teacher's case demonstrates a level of honesty and self-examination in which few teachers are willing to engage. Perhaps some aspect of her insights can be attributed to her maturity and life experiences both in and outside of the home. Her comments about being tired of her "white middle class life," is a recognition of existing social inequities. However, taken out of context, the comment might be misconstrued as a desire for "danger" and "adventure" in the "strange and exotic" environs of the inner city. One of the significant points the teacher makes is that she chose to work in this setting. Unfortunately, many teachers who work in inner-city and/or diverse cultural settings, if given the choice, would choose not to work there.

The teacher points out that nothing in her teacher preparation or orientation readied her for the challenge of her third period. This class has had an intimate relationship with failure and disappointment. Her first day "pep talk" had little impact except to alert the students that they had a push-over for a teacher. They knew they could intimidate her and control the class. In many classrooms where teachers have successfully taught students considered difficult, the teachers jealously guard their privacy on those first few days. Visitors and other outsiders are prohibited from observing as they lay the groundwork. They begin the year by "reading the riot act," making it clear to students that the teacher is in charge and that expectations and standards are high. The teacher's more low key, "middle class" appeal to the students laid a weak foundation. The question of who was to be in charge was unsettled. Immediately, Veronica made a decision to fill the "leadership void." With the help of Travis, Lee, and "Larry Luv," the "junta" had been established. Veronica's note at the end of the period confirmed the teacher's worst fears.

One of the most important statements this teacher makes is, "These students would have been a fearsome group in any color, but their blackness seemed at first to be a barrier." Would that more teachers would confront these racial and cultural taboos! So often we hear teachers giving a standard, pat response of "Oh, I don't see color. I just see children." Racial and cultural differences are a part of the warp and woof of the American social, cultural, and historical fabric. They don't go away in the classroom. Our attempts to ignore these differences in an effort to counteract inequity often serves to widen these gulfs. The teacher did not enter this teaching situation free of some cultural baggage of her own. She was not immune to the perceptions about race (and blackness, in particular) that surround us. When her Gang of Four confirmed some of the stereotypes she may have held, she found it difficult at first to separate their behavior from their blackness. *After* she was able to establish individual relationships with the students, she reflects that their race took on less significance. She discovered a central tenet of multiculturalism — difference does not mean deficit. Acknowledging differences (and the apprehensions we may have about those differences) is a key step in making the classroom a more humane and equitable place for all students.

The teacher could have easily given up in this situation. After all, she had other classes that were working just fine. She could have cut her losses and tried to endure. Instead, she began searching for help. The resources of the school provided her with some temporary relief but her dependence on extrinsic support served to underscore the fact that she was not in charge. Her efforts to learn more about the Gang of Four was a positive step, but she was forced to use what she learned about them in the same way they were using what they knew about her — to intimidate. This created something of a stand-off in the classroom. They weren't losing ground, but they weren't gaining any either. She recognized that nobody, neither she nor the students, was satisfied with the situation.

At this point, the teacher takes her biggest gamble. She decides to be herself, operate in a way in which she was comfortable, *and* tackle the problem. She opens up to the class without appealing for sympathy (which probably would have backfired) and invites them into the analysis and solution of the problem. It is during the students' reports that the teacher returns to a theme that she began early in the case. She expected to learn from the students! Unlike teachers who perceive their work with inner city and diverse cultural students as "missionary" work with the "poor unfortunates," she took this assignment with the expectation that she, too, could learn. This reciprocity is an essential element of successful teaching, particularly with students of different racial and cultural backgrounds. Her students knew what she knew. She was *supposed* to be in charge of the classroom — not the Gang of Four, not the school security force, not the principal, not the staff development expert. The students' participation helped establish a new norm of shared responsibility and clear authority. By having the students participate in this discussion, the teacher made an opening for herself, one in which she could do what not many of us have an opportunity to do, start over. As a part of her fresh start, the teacher learned a wonderful paradox — having the power means not having to exercise it. The students were now clear on who was in charge. They no longer had divided allegiances between the teacher and the Gang of Four. She had found the "win-win" situation that everyone really wanted.

An important footnote to this case concerns learning more about the students. The teacher has done a fine job of learning about the students as individuals, but they are also a part of a historic and cultural tradition, even if they are unaware of it. Teachers who intend to work in diverse cultural settings need greater cultural resources. They need to know more fully the significance of certain traditions and behaviors. When black students engage in "playing the dozens" (name-calling), "signifying" (instigating), or "selling woof-tickets" (intimidating), along with a host of other behaviors, they are unaware of their cultural significance. At the same time, the classroom teacher finds these behaviors threatening and disruptive (which they can be). A better understanding of where they come from and why they are significant can provide both students and teachers with a better understanding and more powerful ways to use student culture as a bridge to school learning.

Karen Desser, Teacher
San Mateo Union High School District

Sooner or later, most teachers are faced with the "war of attrition" described in this piece. This teacher narrates how she successfully resolved this conflict. In doing so, she also touches on an issue that many teachers need to openly consider: How do I approach my students' race?

Her strengths are noteworthy. I applaud her honesty in admitting that she "hated" this class at first. It is indeed difficult to keep student-teacher interactions from entering an emotional arena. Yet this teacher manages to separate her aggravation from her professional judgment. That judgment helps her to recognize that this was a situation that could be altered. She allows them to share the power in the classroom, not so much to let them choose the curriculum, as to demonstrate to them that she values their opinions. This teacher does not mention how many years of teaching experience she has in total, but certainly the combination of that experience, with the maturity of her character, helps her. Yet her adventures with third period testify to the need for specialized inservice to prepare teachers for teaching in new classroom/school environments.

This type of preparation might have alerted her to some of the problems that she encounters. In a sense, I think Veronica does her teacher a great service: Veronica tries to warn her before it is too late that she has adopted a position that isn't going to accomplish the end she has in mind. This teacher assumes that these students would be grateful for her intervention. The problem is that she fails to take into account the patronization inherent in such an approach. After her "pep talk" on the first day, she comments that "someone muttered that the old school was just fine." To the students of this class, this teacher was entering their world, but telling them that she didn't find value in it. If the teacher was truly interested in empowerment, the students reasoned, she needed to learn how to allow them to make their own value judgments. Once the teacher acknowledges this with the cooperative learning groups, the situation relaxes.

It is fitting that she ends her piece with her performance with Larry, Lee, and Travis. After a semester of trying to encourage her students to broaden their horizons, they could now see that she had broadened hers as well. Initially, this teacher was unprepared for the cultural norms third period brought with them. Race and ethnicity bring themes and issues that have the potential to be either rich resources or taboo barriers. Teachers need to be acquainted with the world of their students so that we can help students to analyze their own world and make their own decisions about what they value.

Heather Ramirez (Mellon Fellow) &
Morgan Marchbanks (Irvine Fellow)
Stanford Teacher Education Program

"Fighting for Life in Third Period" provides some examples for positive change in urban high schools. Specifically, the teacher in this case describes an effective means for classroom management. She first utilizes the school's faculty resources and then listens to the voices and concerns of the students in her classroom. We also believe that the teacher accurately diagnoses her "early problems" with race and class, and we recognize an effort to remedy these problems in her "reflection." However, we feel that there are cultural misconceptions which must be addressed. Due to our own cultural experiences as an African-American woman and a Mexican-American woman, we see this case as a vehicle for educating all teachers. It provides us with an opportunity to clear up misconceptions we see everyday which stretch far beyond this one case. For us it calls forth a dominant issue: the way stereotypes affect teacher perception and, in turn, student achievement.

MORGAN MARCHBANKS

As an African-American woman, a student, and a single mother, I was offended by the description of Veronica. She is a stereotypical caricature of a loose black woman. The terms which describe Veronica are offensive: "Stout, black, stuffed into a flame-red dress, Veronica sauntered slowly, insolently past me and took a seat as conspicuously as possible." This disturbing image incorrectly equates her black skin and tight red dress to insolence. I am very familiar with this sexually permissive, "Jezebel" image of the African-American woman — an image as old as this nation. Its pervasiveness, however, does not excuse its use. The stereotype of the "insolent" and sexually permissive black woman continues to limit African-American women.

The description of The Gang of Four is yet another stereotype. On a surface level, the description refers to

the group displaying inappropriate class behavior, but they are also "rapping, dancing" African Americans. Teachers who feel overwhelmed by the vast differences between themselves and a diverse student body are apt to categorize students by ethnicity, cultural practices, and socio-economic status so as to create easily identified groups. But these categories are dangerous as they limit individual potential.

HEATHER RAMIREZ

As a Mexican-American woman, I take issue with the assumptions surrounding the successful Latino student. This is a "top-achieving" student in the classroom, despite the fact the parents do not speak English. Educators often assume that non-English speaking parents hinder the success of their children in school. This is incorrect.

In Latino culture, the family — not the individual — is the social unit. The family is at the heart of Latino culture, and provides the necessary support for the child to excel. The parents may not understand the American school system. Then it becomes the school's duty to inform the family how best to help the student in the classroom.

ROBBED OF HERITAGE

To us, the focus on the racial and cultural differences overshadows the relevant influence of socio-economic disparity in this case. Consequently, the teacher fails to see how "minority" students might be offended by her pep-talk on the "opportunities" available to those who are "qualified." Her inspirational "opportunities" speech rings false to young people who live the day-to-day reality of racial and economic discrimination — despite the fact that the case identifies a problem with race and class issues.

Her "reflections" represent a significant departure from the stereotypes she held in the beginning of the year.

When addressing the issue of race she claims, "as you take these students into your life and heart, you yourself lose all sense of color. They become individuals to you — real people." Essentially, she is concluding that the best way to handle issues of race and ethnicity is to ignore them. As a result of this "blindness," the students then become "real people." This implies that racial and cultural realities must be avoided to allow the teacher to feel comfortable with the students.

"Color blindness" as an ideology strips us of our individual heritage. It robs us of our pride in what makes us special and unique. This ideology also ignores our lifetime struggle with racial and ethnic discrimination. To be blind invalidates this historic struggle of our people and our contributions to the development of this nation. The "color blind" lens does not allow you to see the whole person, but only a bleached-out image of our culturally rich reality.

The case also misinterprets socio-economic issues. The writer blames the students' substandard classroom behavior and performance on "apathy, laziness, and hopelessness," or the "poverty mentality." This label can be a dangerous weapon, even though this teacher did not intend it as such. Society regards it as an inherent characteristic or defective gene, rather than a survival mechanism to escape the harshness of everyday life. Students, for example, hide behind a veil of hopelessness in order to cope with the bleak reality of limited opportunities. Failure to see this limits the educator's expectations of students. Students then lose hope because they do not expect the educator to offer them a means to change their circumstances. As people of color, our own experiences as students make us see inconsistencies in this teacher's "reflections." She is off to a good start; she questions her biases honestly. However, she arrives at unsatisfactory conclusions, ending up inserting class biases for the original race biases. This is somewhat understandable; she comes from a background completely different from that of her students and is groping for some way to understand them.

As educators facing increasingly diverse student populations, we will encounter these same race and class issues. We will need to find ways to integrate diverse elements into the classroom, and create environments where all students succeed. A part of the answer lies in more education about race and class issues. We must also recruit more teachers from these communities and include the local community in the process of educating their youth. Finally, we need to confront biases honestly, and systematically replace them with the knowledge necessary to teach in today's diverse classroom.

Case 7

Drained by One Troubled Child: Did I Help?

Because of problems that developed around a single student, last year proved to be my most difficult one in 30 years of teaching. The situation disrupted the teaching process, confused the students, and frustrated teachers and administrators alike. Unfortunately, it is a scenario familiar to many teachers and one that defies resolution by recognized remedies.

Ours is a school with a very mixed population located in a predominantly black, inner city community. Many children are bused in from other neighborhoods. In 13 years here, I feel I have developed a sound relationship with the community, the parents, and the neighborhood. A Caucasian teacher, I have taught several children from the same families and have gained an understanding and appreciation of their way of life.

Eric, one of my third graders, was the cause of the frustration and disruption. He was a good-looking, nine-year-old black boy who had been retained in first grade because he was below grade level in reading and language. In mathematics, however, he was above average. Eric had been removed from his home because of abuse and was being raised by a very caring grandmother. He attended our school on an out-of-district permit, so that he could walk to the nearby home of a relative and wait to be picked up by his working grandmother. But this arrangement did not work for long, since Eric's behavior seemed too much for the relative to handle. Eric began traveling to and from school, directly from his grandmother's across town.

At the beginning of the school year he was mildly disruptive and often made only a half-hearted attempt to do any independent work. After the holidays, his attitude distinctly changed for the worse. He began coming to school with a chip on his shoulder. He absolutely refused to do any class work; instead, he spent his time harassing the other children. He would close their books while they were working, knock their books and pencils off their desks, write on their papers, crumple up their work, and generally make a nuisance of himself. He did his best to disrupt group lessons by making gestures, pulling faces, and being deliberately noisy. He was easily frustrated, and it did not take much provocation for him to get involved in a fight. One day he knocked another child down and was hitting him with such ferocity that it took me and two other teachers to stop him. In the process I tore the ligaments in my hand.

I wondered if something had happened to trigger the change in Eric. I told him that he was going to have to start trying harder or he would not pass the minimum standards test necessary to go on to the fourth grade. He replied that it didn't matter because he was going to be living with his mother soon, and she said that he wouldn't have to go to school. In talking with his grandmother, I discovered that the court had granted Eric's mother visitation rights. She had indeed made him promises of this kind, which she must have known she would be unable to keep. Could this be the reason for his worsening behavior?

I tried several strategies to help Eric overcome his behavioral problems. I had meetings with his grandmother, who came to school regularly to meet with the principal and me, and who would talk very calmly with Eric, trying to explain how his actions were hindering his academic performance and that of the others in the class. I also referred Eric to our school site committee for evaluation. Moreover, I had weekly conferences with the counselor Eric had been seeing for the past two years and many telephone conferences and meetings with his social worker.

The counselor felt Eric was making progress, slow though it may be. Both the counselor and social worker were sympathetic to my problems in the classroom, but their focus was definitely on Eric and his personal problems. They were unable to give me any insights about dealing with Eric in the classroom. Let them know when I had problems, they said, and they would try to deal with them in therapy.

In the classroom itself I tried many approaches to dealing with Eric's behavior. Whenever possible I tried to find reason to praise him. He reacted to this with braggadocio, possibly to cover his embarrassment. I also gave him praise in private when it was deserved, and this seemed more effective. Another tactic was seating Eric in the front of the room close to my desk. When he started turning around and bothering children in the row behind, I moved him to the back row. Then he would get out of his seat, wander around, and harass other students.

Then I tried working out an individual contract with Eric, under which I would assign him only a small portion of the required assignment and he would do this reduced assignment to the best of his ability. Since he only half-heartedly agreed to this contract, he never held up his part.

My next strategy was to seat Eric next to Ray, a boy he seemed to hold in high regard. Ray was an excellent student with a very well-rounded personality. I had Ray help Eric as much as possible, assigning them many problems to work on together. This experiment was a partial success, since Eric would accept Ray's help on a limited basis.

After a conference with the principal it was decided Eric would be put on a restricted schedule. He would come at the regular time and leave at 11: 30, after reading and language arts. But Eric would refuse to go. Often the principal would have to come and escort him from the building. He would hide and return a short time later, banging on the doors and metal window gratings. Our principal then assigned a large fifth grader to escort him to the bus stop and make sure he got on the bus.

The principal and I suggested that Eric transfer to a school nearer his home. That way he would not have the long trip across the city and it would be easier for his grandmother to come to school for the frequent confer-ences. Both his social worker and counselor resisted this suggestion, saying that Eric liked our school, and they felt changing schools would be just one more way of adding to his problems.

All of the adults working with Eric spent a great deal of time talking with him in an effort to change his attitude. Most often he would be non-communicative during these sessions; he would listen (or tune out) with an enigmatic smile. During one particular session, he was asked by his social worker repeatedly what he was hoping to accomplish with his disruptive behaviors. He mumbled a few "I don't knows" and then blurted out that he wanted to be in fourth grade. His grandmother explained that his friends were generally older; he considered the third graders babies. When asked if he would be willing to work harder to qualify for transfer to a higher grade, Eric just shrugged and became uncommunicative again.

I felt very guilty, especially by the second half of the year. Because of time spent on Eric's problems, the other 29 children in my class had missed the attention I would normally give them. Many instructional periods were disrupted, and because I had to keep the setting very structured, I wasn't able to present lessons the way I normally do. Much of my planning time was spent instead in conferences with Eric's team.

In June, I was notified that Eric had been accepted for placement in a class for the emotionally disturbed in another school for the following school year. Looking back, I feel I should have worked harder to have Eric removed from class, either by having him placed in a special class or transferred to the fourth grade for at least a trial period. I also feel I should have tried to find out more about Eric's background; the people I worked with seemed very reluctant to disclose information about him, other than that he had been an abused child. Perhaps if I had known more of his background I would have understood him better, and would have been better equipped to help him. If I have a similar situation in the future, I'll be quicker to take these steps.

*Gloria Ladson-Billings
University of Wisconsin*

The situation with Eric is more about his personal circumstances than his racial or cultural background. Eric is one more of countless black male students who are slipping through the cracks in our educational and social service systems. The teacher readily admits that although he was below grade level in reading and language, he was *above* average in mathematics. However, the case fails to discuss ways in which the school environment channeled and challenged these skills.

Any one of the specific circumstances Eric faced was enough to cause him difficulty in school — child abuse, separation from his mother, unstable living arrangements, cross-town travel, retention. All of these combined make for a very volatile situation. Eric is angry (wouldn't you be?) and insecure. He is more mature than his classmates and regards his school experience as a punishment.

The teacher tried several conventional strategies for coping with Eric, but it seems clear that Eric was more than she felt she could handle. Eventually, she resorted to having Eric placed on a half-day schedule, a solution that served to make Eric feel even less secure and less a part of the classroom. She was trying to balance her need to teach the other children and attend to Eric, and that might have been a source of the problem. Eric was not a part of this class. What might she have tried that would have given him a chance to be a part of the group?

It may have made sense to send Eric to a fourth grade class for mathematics. He was working above grade level in this area and the fourth graders were his normal age cohorts. It was also apparent that Eric cared about one person — his mother. Perhaps his language and reading experiences needed to be centered on his relationship with his mother. The relationship between him and his mother was apparently disrupted and distorted by the abuse. A substitute relationship needed to be created. Paradoxically, it is that student who is least

attractive or inviting to love who needs loving the most. Eric needed to be touched. He needed an arm around him every day and despite the inevitable resistance, he needed to be hugged. Eric needed some time outside of the classroom, perhaps time that the teacher did not have. Students damaged by traumas such as Eric are expensive. They cost a lot in time, energy, and effort. But, we must ask ourselves whether or not what we are trying to preserve in Eric is worth the cost. What are we trying to save? Some might say we are trying to save a human being. Others, such as myself, think of it as trying to save a nation.

Eric's placement in the class for the emotionally disturbed solved the teacher's problems, but has it solved Eric's? Black children make up 17 percent of the public school population, but constitute 41 percent of the special education population. In cities like New Orleans, black males are 43 percent of the students, but 58 percent of the failures, 65 percent of suspensions, 80 percent of the expulsions, and 45 percent of the dropouts.[4] Three and a half percent of the college population is black, yet black males are 46 percent of the prison population. What is the outlook for Eric's future? Will being in the emotionally disturbed classroom make a positive difference in his life, or will he just be out of everyone's way until he shows up on a street corner or in front of a judge? Somehow, our Erics have got to become our priority. We cannot be satisfied if we lose even one.

---

[4]Ron Harris, "NAACP discusses threat to black American males," *San Francisco Chronicle*, July 10, 1990, p.A-9.

Lynne Zolli, Teacher
San Francisco Unified School District

It is with both anger and sadness that I respond to this case. I am continually amazed at the paradox between what is expected of the elementary classroom teacher and the lack of support given to fulfill those expectations.

Three years ago, I was part of a program quality review team that visited this teacher's school for three days. At that time I was able to observe her class on several occasions. I found her classroom interactive, visually and academically stimulating, and personalized. There was a feeling of unity and high self-esteem among students of diverse ethnicity and ability levels. When I read her account of Eric, I had a feeling of knowing what she'd been through — the hard work, frustration, concern, and most of all, the guilt. What was missing, however, was anger — anger at a system that places all the responsibility on the classroom teacher without support — anger at a system that allows one student to manipulate the teacher, 29 other students, and the "support" staff.

Throughout the years, I have had many students that could be termed "difficult." However, I have had only two that I felt should not be in a regular classroom. Eric would probably have made three. I knew that this teacher had gone above and beyond her responsibilities to both help and accommodate Eric, but a regular classroom setting was not meeting his needs. Eric was not the teacher's failure. The strategies she employed to help Eric within the classroom, in conjunction with the regular, ongoing contacts with his grandmother, counselor, social worker, and school personnel would have made inroads with many students with behavior problems. Eric needed more, and the teacher could no longer meet those needs.

Successful classroom teachers at the elementary school level often have one thing in common. They feel they should be able to handle any and every situation despite the obstacles. As a result, they trip over their own success and can end up with immeasurable frustration and guilt over "their" failures. In this teacher's case, Eric would have never received placement in a special education class without her initial referral and continual input. Instead of feeling a sense of accomplishment, relief, or at least anger at the amount of energy she had to expend during the school year, the teacher was filled with guilt — she hadn't done enough, she should have tried harder.

I believe that education is a basic right for all children, but the educational setting must be appropriate. It is not a question of blaming Eric for his disruptive behavior or his physical violence. He was not functional at that point in time in the regular classroom. It is important to have safeguards in the system to prevent abusive labeling and improper placement of students. Likewise, it is important to not let those safeguards bog down necessary placements for those students with special needs.

Teaching is not easy, but it provides rewards and a great sense of accomplishment when we know we have made a difference. There is, however, a danger in believing that we are responsible for making that difference in every student who comes into our classrooms. We must realize when we are unable to meet a student's needs, and not personalize it as our own failure. If we as teachers are to value and respect ourselves, we must draw the line at what we are expected to contend with and free ourselves of the guilt that permeates formidable and perplexing situations.

Bettye C. Haysbert, Staff Developer
San Francisco Unified School District

The teacher seemed genuinely concerned about the welfare of the student and attempted solutions through normal channels. I agree with her statement, "This is a familiar scenario and one that defies resolution by *recognized* remedies." I would add, "and *commonly used* remedies." Our remedies are rendered ineffective because they are not designed to address the real problem — "hurting children."

The teacher reports the problem with the student as one that occurs in the classroom (disrupting class, etc.). Yet, when she sought a solution, exterior elements (grandmother, counselors, principal, another class placement, etc.) became the focus. Not one of the attempted solutions focused on the teacher and her interaction with the student or other dynamics in the classroom.

One way I have addressed this sort of issue is to first recognize that I have a hurting child who needs to be shown that he or she is truly cared for. I verbally assure by giving praise often, followed with such action as having frequent one-on-one short talks, hugs, and touches (hand, arm, shoulder). Class conversations and problem-solving time are integral parts of the class routine. Limits are set and clearly communicated, as are consequences, in case he or she chooses not to work within the stated limits. I remain consistent and fair in all dealings, especially when the child tests the limits (which is sure to happen).

African-American students (especially males) are very sensitive to the feelings, attitudes, and behavior of people in their environment. When they receive negative messages, they will respond in the best way they know how— by behaving in self-protective ways to save face. At these times, teachers can ask themselves the following questions: What attitudes, beliefs, and expectations do I hold toward this child? How do I communicate them to him and my class and how does that influence student/student and student/teacher interactions? This is critical, because students will imitate behavior modeled by the teacher.

An alarming situation exists among African-American children. They make up the highest percentage of students in special education classes. Most such students are males, with white female teachers making the highest number of referrals. Clearly, there is cause for concern. Preparing teachers for effective teacher/student interactions means looking at teacher training in new ways.

Ideally, teacher training should include:

- Affective education.

- Supportive techniques for children who are hurting — regardless of the hurt's source. Details of the situation sometimes become excuses — reasons why teachers can't help. Having more information could be potentially dangerous if used unwisely. Skills are needed, and skills are not gained from an accumulation of information.

- Methods of teaching social skills so that students will learn acceptable behaviors.

- Conflict management/resolution skills, including listening, communicating, problem solving, and decisionmaking.

- Opportunities for introspection so that teachers can honestly assess their attitudes, beliefs, and expectations about African-American students and think about how those are communicated.

- Suggestions for establishing a routine forum where students can speak to issues that concern them.

- Classroom observations and teacher feedback on classroom dynamics (identifying supportive or non-supportive ways of interacting).

We are constantly receiving students whose backgrounds and needs are very different from our own and from those we have been trained to address. Thus our old methodologies are ineffective. We blame the victim to compensate for our own lack of skills. This is a perfect example of how a problem for the teacher becomes a problem for the child, one with potentially life-long repercussions.

EPILOGUE

Case Writer — Six Months Later

Since writing this case, I have had another student who was as disruptive as Eric. Again, this was a black male from an abusive home. He had been placed in a series of foster homes. Again, this child was behind in his academic studies and had been retained one year in first grade.

I am beginning to seriously question the practice of retaining youngsters in the elementary grades. I particularly question retaining black males. This seems to be a substantial blow to their self-esteem. Not only are they older than their classmates, but often they're far larger, too. Socially, they don't fit in with the younger children in their class.

Both of these boys needed one-to-one instruction in reading and language arts. They needed to be on an individual contract whether they were in third grade or fourth. I realize they would still have many of the same problems if they hadn't been retained, but I think their classroom behavior wouldn't have been as serious if they were in the proper grade for their age, working with peers with whom they were better able to socialize.

Case 8

Darius: I Hope He Makes It!

I have taught intermediate grades for 25 years in strictly inner-city, multi-racial settings. I teach there because that's where I, a mixed minority teacher,[5] grew up. I have always worked with at-risk children because I know them best. My current school is targeted for special funding due to our high number of low-achieving, at-risk-of-failure students.

Darius — a black nine-year-old — spent third and fourth grades on half-day. This schedule was agreed upon by teacher, administrator, and family; since he created so many violent problems during the school morning, he could go home at lunchtime every day. His third grade teacher smugly told me that they had a bargain: he didn't mess with Darius, and Darius didn't mess with him. What that might mean scared me. I know it meant he didn't do anything he didn't really want to do. His fourth grade teacher said he was a good reader, so she had him read all morning with different groups until he got bored. When disruptive, he ended up in the office until sent home at lunch. On the yard, he hurt others to the point where he wasn't allowed on the yard most of the time.

When the principal told me she wanted me to take Darius for fifth grade, I was not thrilled. I'd just had the school's most serious behavior problem for two-and-a-half years and thought I deserved a break. I tried to beg off, but the sly dear reminded me of my success with darling Andre and other problem children. I teach conflict resolution in my classroom, which mainly consists of words, phrases, and sentences kids can say instead of using their old abusive problem-solving methods, and I've had a high rate of success with at-risk children. We work a lot with a thing called "active listening" — putting yourself in another's place and getting to the real meaning of what is going on with each other.

---

[5]The case author's ethnic background is Native American and white, and she was raised in a Latino community.

Since I literally saw the writing on the wall, I started talking with Darius. He had been teacher-nominated to be one of my Conflict Managers,[6] and during the three-day training had been very observant and thoughtful. I found him a particularly bright and insightful child. He knew he was behind grade level, even though he had been praised for his reading. I hoped the program would help him articulate his feelings. But Darius quit the program early because he refused to show up for duty and was bullying people rather than helping them solve their problems. I also learned that he could barely add and subtract and that his "great" reading was two solid years below grade level.

When his fourth grade teacher told him he would be in my room for fifth grade, he cut class to come tell me the good news. I said, "Well, you know, I'm gonna make a deal with you, you know, like the others did. Mine's a little different though, because I've seen you in Conflict Manager training and I know just how smart you really are. I heard you haven't done much learning the last few years. If you want to work with me, you have to do just that: work. Over the summer I want you to memorize the times tables and remember the Conflict Manager stuff, you know, the rules. As for me, I will never, never send you home and you will stay with me all day, not half-day, and you will have to work with me and the class to solve any problems you have with us." He just

---

[6]Conflict Managers is a program that teaches children conflict-resolution skills such as listening, repeating what you hear, reading people's body language, how to make a good resolution, and basically how to say what you feel without screaming, shouting, and name-calling. It is taught through skits where children act out scenarios based upon their own experiences and gives them the opportunity to brainstorm alternative solutions to everyday problems. After completing training, they circulate in pairs on the schoolyard and are available if people need them. They are sworn to strict confidentiality and are completely trustworthy.

looked at me and said, "Okay." I wonder now if I'd only set myself up for failure.

During the summer I ran into Darius and his aunt at Mervyn's buying school clothes. He ran up to me, hugged me, and made me ask him some times tables. He remembered and was keeping his end of the deal.

The year started great. Darius did most, not all, of the classwork. He got along in class marginally. He had a dickens of a time working in the tribes (a method utilizing cooperative learning groups); he wouldn't bow to the group process, and he annoyed his neighbors, but there were not many abuses and outright fights. He actually got relaxed enough so that I could hug him and get a hug back. One time he let me actually flip him over and tickle him. He'd seen me do that to Marco and thought it looked like fun; it made me realize he hadn't been played with much as a baby. He still got into trouble on the yard at recess and at lunch.

I informed the administrators that what he did on the yard should not affect his classroom time or mine. For a while they held to this; he got other consequences for breaking school rules at recess and at lunch. Then one day, he got in a horrible fight and was suspended for three days. I wasn't asked for my input and, in fact, I didn't know about the incident and subsequent suspension until after school.

When he got back after the suspension, he was a different child. He openly argued and fought with classmates. He refused to do any class work and threw his papers on the floor in front of me, daring me to do something about it. It was open and total hostility for over two weeks. I asked him in front of the class what was wrong and said I didn't like the way he was behaving. He glared at me and calmly said, "I don't care because I hate you, you fat bitch." I asked him to leave the room to cool off a while. He just glared at me again and sat there. I took the rest of the class out and asked the Elementary Advisor to go in and talk to him. When I brought the

class back in, she said he was madder than hell at me. He said I was a liar and then refused to say any more. Then I remembered the bargain. He had kept his part and I had not kept mine. Even though the office suspended him, I had not defended him. He didn't make a distinction about who had done the suspending. He only knew this wasn't what he had bargained for. I sat down next to him and apologized. I said the vice-principal, not I, suspended him. He said that didn't matter, I was a liar. I was thinking fast and furiously and didn't know what to do, so I just said I made a bad mistake. Could he please give me a second chance? I would deal with the office and try to make them understand what our problem was. He wouldn't look at me for the longest time, then mumbled, "Okay." He was aloof for a few days, then all of a sudden handed in a stack of old work papers and stories. That was his peace offering.

For a couple of weeks all went well. Then Darius started arguing with classmates and getting into fights in the classroom. I figured he was testing me, so I let him slide. I arranged conflict-resolution skits to help him resolve some of his problems and gave him positive reinforcement whenever possible. Two months have gone by and he has never returned to his previous good behavior. I don't know if he will. I don't know if I can live up to his personal code. Darius has given me a strong reminder of how children hold you to your word, no matter what.

EPILOGUE

One month after this writing, Darius's mother was murdered. Needless to say, he regressed. Interestingly enough, he is becoming affectionate again. I think he learned something, or maybe he just needs us. The class and I are working to be there for him.

Gloria Ladson-Billings
University of Wisconsin

Darius's situation (like that of Eric in "Drained by One Troubled Child") involves the youngster's personal circumstances as much as his racial/cultural background. This teacher makes a statement in her first paragraph that I find puzzling. She describes herself as a "mixed minority." By failing to be more specific about her own identification,[7] is she drawing closer or farther away from her students? Does her "mixed minority" status give her cultural knowledge that she uses while working with students? The overwhelming number of black people in America are "mixed," but their identification is with their blackness.

The teacher's strength in this situation is her willingness to act as an advocate for children. She knew Darius would be assigned to her classroom, and although she balked initially, she took some proactive steps toward dealing with him. Being assigned the most difficult youngsters is not an unusual occurrence for teachers who are successful with black students. Instead of using these teachers as resources for assisting other teachers in dealing with difficult students, administrators often make these teachers' classrooms dumping grounds — they do, that is, until these teachers rebel or burn out.

This teacher demonstrated her knowledge of an important aspect of working with black students: cultivating a relationship. That relationship is not to be misconstrued as "making friends" — an approach tried by many young white teachers, which often ends in disaster. She did what she saw as necessary to acknowledge Darius's individuality and special circumstances. She was clear about her expectations and her responsibilities. Darius confirmed his understanding and acceptance of their relationship when he hugged her in the department store and insisted on reciting his times tables. This teacher

[7] We identified this teacher's ethnic background in the case *after* Ladson-Billings wrote this commentary.

further cemented the relationship by her willingness to maintain physical contact with him through tickling and playful flipping. All of these behaviors on the teacher's part showed her understanding that equality in the classroom (just like in a family) is not necessarily "sameness." She wanted each of the students to be successful but she recognized that their individual needs required different approaches.

The teacher's relationship with Darius began to unravel when the school administration suspended him. Darius, like many youngsters, perceived the teacher to be fully in control. Thus, when he was suspended, his anger was specifically directed at the teacher. Darius had not had good relationships with his previous teachers. They tolerated him — to a point. They were happy to get rid of him via the half-day schedule. They lied to him, telling him he was performing at higher reading levels than he actually was. This teacher represented someone who saw past his faults, and when he thought she let him down, he was devastated.

This case does not reveal much about the origins of Darius's problems, but the epilogue, which tells of his mother's murder, helps us to understand that there is a lot of trauma in this youngster's life. The school can only respond to some of his needs. Unfortunately, if he does not have other teachers like this one, who are willing to work hard to develop a special relationship with him, his school-based needs will not be met either. As he grows older, his presence as a black male will be perceived as more threatening. Without a sincere effort to encourage his talents and see his potential as a learner, he is likely to end up in the pile of disturbing statistics concerning black males. For Darius's sake, I hope that the teacher's efforts pay off. For the sake of all the Dariuses to come, I hope that this teacher will have the opportunity to share her skills and insights throughout her school.

Peg Foley Reynolds, Teacher
San Francisco Unified School District

The first thought that comes to mind in reading this case is the frustration teachers face because of circumstances beyond their control, especially in dealing with those students with severe emotional or behavioral problems. It's hard to imagine what more the teacher could have done to help Darius solve his problems. Perhaps if she had commented on consultations she must have had with Darius's family, an important clue might have pinpointed a serious deprivation in his upbringing and explained his readiness to distrust adults.

However, I did get a message from this case that is very important. We, as teachers, have to be very careful what we promise children when bargaining or making a deal with them. We must make sure that we have the authority and the opportunity to carry out our end of the bargain. In Darius's case, the teacher could have made sure that he understood that she had limited control over what happened outside the classroom.

This teacher should not be too hard on herself concerning this situation; there seem to be many factors contributing to Darius's problems. It's possible he used the fact that she had not kept her side of the bargain as an easy way to explain behavioral problems he did not understand himself. If he is going to have success in the future, I feel that at this stage Darius is going to need in-depth counseling, perhaps even to the extent of placing him in a residential care program.

Case 9

A Trip to Hell

After seven years in the classroom, I figured I could handle most teaching challenges. I had taught classes with 34 or more students; I had taught fourth and fifth graders with distress patterns so profound that spontaneous fights would break out, with furniture kicked or thrown; I have had classes where 20 percent of the students had been identified as learning disabled; I've taught a fifth grade where students ranged in age from nine to 13 and in mass from 50 to over 200 pounds. But this pull-out Spanish class of 13 Latino fifth graders blew the top off of the instructional expertise and management skills I had gained.

Our inner-city school is located in an historically Asian neighborhood. Among its 800 students, the main cultural groups are Asian. Latino students (40 percent of our population) are largely bused in from other parts of the city. In my capacity as a resource teacher, I stepped in as a temporary pull-out sub for a teacher out on medical leave for a number of weeks.

Despite my small group's reputation for being demanding and acting out, I expected little trouble engaging them for 50 minutes daily. In fact, I saw this as an opportunity. Our district had been unable to provide us with enough fully credentialed bilingual teachers and paraprofessionals. The Spanish bilingual class was full, as was the English Language Development (ELD) class, in which English is almost exclusively the medium of instruction. These fifth graders — because of their high proficiency in English — had been placed in a Chinese bilingual class in which content was delivered mostly in English (Cantonese-speaking students were given language support as needed). Because we are a "maintenance bilingual program," for one hour daily all students in this class were provided primary language instruction: while 13 students were studying Chinese with their classroom teacher, 13 were with me studying Spanish. Keep in mind that these are students whose learning styles incline them to excel when presented with determined, lively interaction with the teacher. They do best with much validation on an intimate,

personal level, and they generally appreciate appropriate, sincere physical contact, such as hugs.

Terms of endearment, as well, are an integral part of our language and culture when addressing one another: *corazón, mi amor, mi rey, mi hijita* are among the many expressions used every day when we speak with children at home. (The direct translations into English are awkward and do not convey the sentiment in the way it is conveyed in Spanish: heart, my love, my king, my daughter.) Teachers from the culture often tend to feel comfortable using such expressions in class, and students are of course familiar with them.

Such endearments are not common in Chinese or Chinese-American households, and certainly less so in the public school setting. My belief is that this small yet significant cultural discrepancy influences the learning that goes on in the classroom. This group of students also feels that there is favoritism happening on the part of their teacher towards the Chinese students. As a Filipino/Chicano deeply committed to bilingual education throughout the elementary years, I felt I could create the time and space for these youngsters to be validated — culturally, linguistically, and personally. I am also trained in conflict resolution, both for adults and children, am well-liked and respected by students, and — especially for this group — consider myself a student role model.

My first class with these 13 students was a trip to hell. I had prepared several activities. For example, I planned a 20-question game where one child would leave the room while the others wrote down a Spanish word. We would then tape the word to the returning student's back, and he/she would try to guess it by asking 20 questions.

To say that the students sabotaged the game is an understatement. They were on top of tables, under tables. They threw books. They fought. And at every opportunity, they screamed obscenities and put-downs at one another. At least half spoke continually. Two cried. And all refused to speak Spanish. I was not surprised at their resistance — it is not an uncommon occurrence with Latino students. But what shocked me was its intensity.

Devastating as that session was, I got one tiny insight. Somehow, in the last 10 minutes of the period, discussion drifted to how a classmate of these students had once smashed her hand in the classroom door. As the language became more descriptive, i.e., more grotesque, students became more attentive, enthused, creative. I immediately thought of a homework assignment: prepare and be ready to tell about a time when YOU had been hurt. Use as many descriptive words as you can. Great idea! But it was another humiliating failure. None of them did it.

In the days that followed, I decided to focus on the students' low self-esteem. I decided to try a series of strategies. I started pulling students individually from their classroom, one student daily, for the 20 minutes before Spanish class. I would ask that person for input into that day's lesson — in other words, let him or her share the planning. Speaking in both languages — common with bilingual/bicultural people — I would ask him or her to carry materials to the pull-out room and to pick others to perform certain tasks. And I spent time counseling and validating, listening to the student's version of what makes school hard or unpleasant, and gently — but firmly — restating my expectations of him or her for that afternoon's class.

I send validation letters to students, typed on official school district stationery. I put my arm around them as we walk to class, and I use terms of endearment. I tell them how intelligent they are and occasionally call them (not their parents) on the phone in the evening to talk. I respect their natural autonomy and intrinsic motivation for learning and achievement. And I feel almost great about the positive changes I've seen develop as a result of these efforts.

Academic instruction, however, has been a disappointment. Though I have ambitions of presenting an innovative, cultural, and literature-based curriculum, I have resorted to using dittos. Some activities involve cutting and pasting exercises to help teach rudimentary Spanish phonics and spelling. Others are short stories written in Spanish. As the term went on, I made the jump to our basal reader. I found that this group responded favorably to having the "official" yardstick of progress: the basal. In part, I am trying to build teamwork. And I've stacked the cards so that the students are likely to succeed — at least in an immediate sense.

Even though I moved the two most attentive and least demanding students to a different Spanish class, the group seems quieter, probably happier. But it feels as if I've watered down the curriculum by providing relatively unchallenging, too-elementary assignments.

Now, after five weeks with these children, their regular classroom teacher has commented that some of them have been turning in more work. I believe they are beginning to feel that I truly care about and respect them. I even received a valentine from Roberto — even though two days earlier I had sent him out of the room for pushing all my buttons and yelling "Dogface!" at another student. Most important, I am getting a sense that these students are beginning to feel invested in the class.

Still unanswered, and still bothersome to me, however, is why these children were so angry, so hostile. Did I evoke this? Their regular Spanish teacher is a mother figure with the nurturing patience of the kindergarten teacher that she is (and in fact, many of these were ex-students of hers). Perhaps they felt abandoned. If I have another similar challenge, I'll be more careful to outline my expectations, increase communication with parents, identify our goals — academically and socially — and take advantage of student input on how to reach these goals.

Richard Piper, Director
California Learning Designs, Inc.

I wish to focus my remarks on three topics: the students, the program, and the interaction between the two. First, the students.

It is instructive to note that the students come to the pull-out teacher with a "reputation for being demanding and acting out." They immediately live up to the reputation, screaming obscenities and put-downs at one another, throwing books, and fighting. The teacher seeks a reason for the anger and hostility. "Did I evoke this?" he asks.

The answer is almost certainly "No!" Rather, what we see here is an example of what Freire calls *horizontal violence* (defined as the violence of oppressed peoples directed against one another). It is only one of six characteristics of oppressed peoples. The other five are:

1)   fatalistic attitudes

2)   self-depreciation

3)   self-distrust

4)   magical belief in the power of the oppressor

5)   feel like property.

There is neither time nor space here to expand on Freire's brilliant analysis of the effects of oppression on the oppressed, but there is little doubt that his analysis is one of the answers to the teacher's question.

Then there is the issue of *language*. The teacher says that these students ". . . because of their high proficiency in English, had been placed in a Chinese bilingual class where English is the medium of instruction." In fact, there is little evidence in the anecdote that these students actually had high proficiency in English (if by "high" proficiency is

meant that their ability to understand, speak, read, and write English equals the expectancies associated with fifth grade native speakers of English). Educators often mistake surface fluency for real proficiency.

The real reasons for the placement in a Chinese bilingual class are probably the following:

1)   Desegregation concerns mandated assignment to a school in a Chinese neighborhood (the teacher mentions that 40 percent of the students are Latino, a figure that probably corresponds to the quota for Latinos in the school).

2)   The Spanish bilingual class at the school was full and there were no other teachers at the school who could be assigned to teach another fifth-grade Spanish bilingual class. The same holds for the English Language Development option.

The teacher goes on to say that, ". . . all refused to speak Spanish." Such a refusal is common among Latino students and is probably due to social pressure on the one hand and declining Spanish language proficiency on the other. The clear evidence from evaluation studies of bilingual programs is that Latino students enter kindergarten and first grade with levels of Spanish language proficiency that rivals the proficiency of same-age students in Latin American countries, but that by the fifth grade, parity with same-grade peers in Latin American countries is lost.

The teacher notes, finally, that the students were ". . . speaking in both languages." Presumably, the teacher is referring to the use of both languages in a single communication, a practice technically known as code-switching. There are Latino scholars who believe that code-switching has important social value for the speakers. This is probably true. It is also true that bilinguals who have full control over two language systems seldom code-switch. Conversely, code-switchers seldom have full control over two language systems. In the present case, we are almost certainly dealing with students who have limited proficiency in both languages. The code-switching in which they engage serves not only as a cultural statement, but also as a clear sign of language limitations.

What we have here, then, is a group of students who are progressively losing proficiency in their primary language while at the same time failing to make expected progress in the acquisition of English. They are becoming double limited bilinguals.

We turn now to the question of self-image. The teacher senses that this may be a problem because he places so much emphasis on building esteem through cultural affirmation. He uses culturally based terms of endearment, culturally accepted hugging, one-on-one contacts, validation letters, and Spanish as means for cultural, linguistic, and personal "validation."

The teacher also notes that "This group of students . . . feels that there is favoritism happening on the part of their teacher towards the Chinese students." It is important to understand that to the perceiver, perceptions are "fact." Whether factual or not, the perception undercuts the students' confidence in themselves, leading to what Freire calls self-depreciation and self-distrust. These two factors parallel the horizontal violence discussed above.

In summary, we have looked at the students' horizontal violence, their use of language (both English and Spanish) and their self-image. We turn now to some observations about the *program*.

The teacher professes ". . . ambitions of presenting an innovative, literature-based curriculum." This is a laudable goal and is consistent with the direction of language curriculum in California. That is not where the teacher started, however. He began "feeling out" the students with language games like 20 Questions in Spanish. This failed. The teacher then went to language experiences based on the students' personal experiences.

This failed also, both as an in-class activity and as a homework activity.

Temporarily abandoning the literature-based curriculum, the teacher went to the tried and true time burner — dittos. It's easy to keep kids quiet and on task. Unfortunately, the dittos did not involve language acquisition activities (which the students need) so much as metalinguistic activities (important but, for these students, premature). Then came the basals — predictable and comfortable. We are not told whether the basals were grade level, but for most of the students they were probably not. In concluding his remarks on the curriculum, the teacher states, ". . . it feels as if I've watered down the curriculum by providing relatively unchallenging, too-elementary assignments."

Did the teacher have any alternatives to this distressing set of curriculum decisions? What should one do with bilingual students whose language proficiency is well below grade level in both languages? This is a question about the interaction of the language minority student and the instructional program, our third topic.

The tried and true response to the question is based on the language mismatch hypothesis, a hypothesis which attributes the school failure of large numbers of language minority students to the fact that the language and culture of the student and the language and culture of the school do not match. Under these conditions, one of four solutions is possible.

1) Require the student to acquire the language and culture of the school before being allowed into regular classes. This is the ESL-only solution.

2) Require the school to use the language and culture of the child for academic instruction until such time as the student, through structured English language instruction (including ESL and sheltered English), acquires enough English to succeed in a regular classroom. This is the transitional bilingual solution.

3) Require the school to immerse both the language minority and language majority students in the other's language. This must be done under careful conditions. It is the bilingual immersion solution.

4) Require the school to use a combination of ESL and sheltered English until such time as the student acquires enough English to succeed in a regular class. This is the sheltered solution.

The first option has generally proven to be unsuccessful. The other three have all proven to be successful as long as they are matched appropriately to the student population and as long as they are properly implemented. The program illustrated in the present case study is closest to option 2.

Everything done by the teacher was based on the language mismatch hypothesis. How did he do? The strongest part of the teacher's approach was the cultural affirmation approach. Also commendable was the intent to implement a literature-based approach. Unfortunately, the students were not linguistically up to something as rigorous as this. From that point on, the program began falling apart.

What went wrong? First, it is likely that the students' Spanish had become so weak that it was virtually unusable as a vehicle for learning. Second, even if this were not true, the students' rejection of the language would suggest its abandonment as a vehicle for learning. The sheltered solution would have been preferable.

This is not to say that developing real strength in one's primary language is not important or valuable. On the contrary, in the best of all possible worlds, all students would become bilingual. However, in the absence of serious intent to develop real proficiency in option 1, using the language as a means of instruction once adequate proficiency has been lost is a waste of time. The students in this case study match this profile.

Once the sheltered option is adopted, procedures are well known, so there is no use spending time or space describing them.

In this case study, it is important to recognize that the language mismatch hypothesis was the operational hypothesis guiding all that the teacher did. It is also important to recognize that the treatment based on the hypothesis was imperfectly conceived and implemented. Even so, it is worth asking a final question. Would it have made any real difference if the treatment had been perfectly conceived and implemented?

There is increasing evidence that the mismatch hypothesis is incapable of explaining all the data that are coming in from bilingual education research and evaluation. There are plenty of examples of language minority students who are thrown into sink-or-swim situations and thrive. There are even more examples of students who are carefully placed in linguistically well-conceived programs and fail. Without giving up on the hard-won gains of the past 20 years, we must now admit that it will take additional hypotheses to account for the variety of outcomes that are seen.

One such hypothesis is, what (for lack of agreed-upon terminology) we shall call the empowerment hypothesis. Underlying this hypothesis is the assumption that some children grow up in circumstances that result in their disempowerment. Such circumstances can be called oppression. Freire defines such circumstances as follows:

> Any situation in which "A" objectively exploits "B" or hinders his pursuit of self-affirmation as a responsible person is one of oppression. Such a situation in itself constitutes violence, even when sweetened by false generosity, because it interferes with man's ontological and historical vocation to be more human.

This theme has been picked up by Cummins in his book *Education for Empowerment* and by Ogbu and Matute-

Bianchi in *Beyond Language: Social and Cultural Factors in Schooling Language Minority Students.* The importance of these books, together with that of Freire (*Pedagogy of the Oppressed*) is that they place part of the locus for the problems described in the present case study both inside and outside of the school. Teachers need not carry the whole burden for the kinds of behavior and lack of proficiency that many language minority students exhibit. These books are also important because all three contribute to an understanding of what educators might do in order to address the problems that have their roots not so much in pedagogy as in objective situations of oppression.

Amado Padilla
Stanford University

In reading this case, I agonized over the Latino students who were the subjects. In addition, I felt uneasy for the Filipino/Chicano teacher, the Chinese bilingual class-mates, the families of Latino students caught in the web of equal educational opportunity, teachers and adminis-trators trapped in a dilemma that obscures their profes-sionalism, and a society that doesn't seem to know quite what to do about the student diversity of our schools. The case was troubling as much for what it did not say as for what it said.

Let me begin, then, with a bias of my own because it is at the center of what I found troubling about this case. I think we make a serious mistake when minority stu-dents are bused from other parts of a city to a school where minority students of another background are located, especially where this is done simply to achieve some sort of arbitrary court-mandated ethnic balance. If some educational goal were the basis for such busing (e.g., to attend a foreign language magnet school), then fine, but not when Latino students are used to achieve ethnic balance in a Chinese bilingual school, which appears to be the situation in this case report. Thus, I find myself wishing to be the advocate for the Latino students because of their academic plight. These stu-dents seem to me to be pawns in a game that in no way is intended to benefit them.

I interpret the students' behavior as anger directed at their school environment. And who wouldn't be angry? Here they are bused away from home, with a Chinese teacher who likely favors their Chinese counterparts, and a resource teacher who is substituting for the regular teacher and who is not sure what to do for the one hour a day he has them for Spanish. I find myself annoyed with the absence of a rationale for why the students have Spanish instruction in the first place. The author of the case states that the students were "... all very proficient in English." I wonder why the students were receiving instruction in Spanish, rather than more instruction in mathematics or science. Certainly, I hope the instruction in Spanish was not a pretext for calling what was being done a Spanish bilingual program.

I also worry about the lack of attention to the vast heterogeneity that exists among Hispanic students. To be informed that the students are all Latino is, I suppose, better than not knowing anything about the students, but just barely. It may be a lot to ask of teachers, but nonetheless, it is important to know if the Latino children were born in this country or if they are immigrants. I would want to know exactly how proficient the students were in English. I would probably even want to know something about the conditions under which they learned English. It is also important to know the educational level of the parents and from where in Latin America the parents originate. Simply because two individuals are Latino does not imply that they should get along well with each other. There are deep historical, cultural, and political divisions between many different countries in Latin America, just as there are between Northern Ireland and England, Israel and Palestinians, or Korea and Japan. So why should we become alarmed when Latinos periodically scream obscenities at each other! What is this misperception educators have that leads them to believe that all Latino students should get along, especially in a city like San Francisco that has such a heterogeneous Hispanic population? We don't need to unravel complicated social theories of "horizontal violence" or oppression to explain the classroom behavior of the Latino students.

My impression is that this teacher's assumption about Latino youngsters may be faulty. I offer this suggestion based on the case. For instance, unless I knew the students well, I would not presume that somehow they were culturally "set" to hear terms of endearment as the author states. In fact, I would be particularly cautious on this point for two primary reasons. By the fifth grade, the use of *mi hijita, corazón,* etc. could be very embarrassing to the student, especially when delivered by a

stranger. Further, I would be concerned about the cross-sex appropriateness of such terms and how they could be misinterpreted by pre-adolescents! It may be that the teacher's use of terms of endearment actually backfired on him and interfered with his interactions with students.

I am reminded of the film *Stand and Deliver*. In the film, we see very vividly that the teacher, Jaime Escalante, did not employ endearments to win his students over; rather, he used barrio humor, often poking jokes at the students as well as at himself. Further, he challenged his students. He asked them whether they had the *ganas* to excel in mathematics. He demanded work. He didn't stand by uttering, "Okay, *mis hijitos,* it's time to do our math problem." "Oh, *mi corazón,* please look this way." The use of these kinds of endearments with Hispanic students is exaggerated and probably inappropriate, except with very young children. The author of this case may underestimate the social and intellectual development of his students when he discusses the employment of endearments as a viable strategy with all Hispanic youngsters. While emotional and affective support are important, exaggerated endearments perpetuate one of those meaningless stereotypes that have crept into what is nowadays being termed multicultural education.

In this same vein, I find the discussion of the Latino students' self-esteem very superficial. It is obviously true that some Latino students may have lower self-esteem than other students their age, but to arrive at such a generalized conclusion implies a lack of familiarity with Latino students. The wholesale belief that all underachieving minority students have low self-esteem is perpetuated by well-meaning teacher educators who don't bother to inquire about what psychologists mean by self-esteem, how it is measured, and whether the construct has applicability in the school context, at least in the way that it is used so often with Latino and other minority students.

My feeling is that the teacher has not been able to work beyond the bounds of his training and is not really seeing the reality of the situation from the students' perspective. In my view, the students are most likely coping very well with a very stressful situation that involves busing to an unfamiliar community and school, teachers who show favoritism to other students, and a teacher who, despite good intentions, is inadvertently as much part of the problem as everything else in the school. If we actually listened to the students involved in this case, they might very well say that each day seemed like "a trip to hell" to them, too. We're more knowledgeable today about the relationship between stress and coping and psychological wellness. The Latino students were probably very stressed and coped in the best way they knew how. We should give them credit for what they endure in school, rather than finding words to describe their anti-school behaviors. Frankly, these students demonstrate a remarkable amount of resilience to survive a schooling experience that most middle class parents would not condone for their own children, but which we find acceptable for minority youngsters.

I was also amazed that the teacher believed that in a few short weeks (and hours) he could turn the Latino students' academic achievement around. On what basis did the teacher believe, because of his familiarity with Latino students and deep commitment to bilingual education, that a few hours with them would reverse what appeared to be their poor scholastic ability? Even though the teacher was most likely on the right track with his program of validating students' learning experiences, co-planning his lessons with them, and making them feel that he truly cared about whether they learned by calling them in the evening, all of this may have been insufficient in the short time that he had the students. Changes in behavior take time, especially in a situation where the students have many negative experiences and deficiencies to overcome.

In sum, this case illustrates the very long way that educators need to go before we truly know how to handle student diversity in our schools. In the case description, we have the image of an individual wishing to work with Latino students who falls prey to many of the same stereotypes and misconceptions concerning Latino students that are so evident in journal articles, texts, and in the "folk wisdom" carried around by practitioners and teacher trainers. With this shortcoming as context, we have social policies that even though well intentioned, create new and often insurmountable problems for minority students. In this case, there are many victims. Certainly, the Latino students are denied their right to a good education, but the teacher is also victim to the complex interplay of wanting to do good and not being able to because of factors outside of his or anyone else's control. Ultimately, society pays the price for students who lose their desire to learn. Regrettably, many of these students will become alienated from school and from the majority society. Yet ironically, they will remain painfully tied to that society because they rely on it for their prosperity.

Lori Murakami and Anna Yamaguchi, Teachers
San Francisco Unified School District

Language minority students must be placed in the proper bilingual classrooms in order for them to achieve success and to have a sense of well-being in school. This teacher's case study is a powerful example of what can occur when students are misplaced and there is a lack of sensitivity to students' bilingual needs.

The teacher tried many alternative strategies, and he went through difficult times with his students in search of one technique that would work the best. The teacher validated their self-worth by allowing individual student input into daily lessons and encouraged them to assume responsibilities. He took interest in their personal lives as well as their school work. Students were listened to, understood, but always reminded of the teacher's expectations. Though the assignments were not as challenging and innovative as the teacher would have liked, they were structured so that the students were able to find success and feel happy about themselves.

What was noticeable in this study was the depth of caring and respect the teacher gave to his students. He invested time and love into them, and in return, the students began to feel the same towards him and towards school. Moreover, he was able to take a small group, give them more attention, and deal with individual needs and problems. This allowed the teacher to develop a positive working relationship with his students. When the student to teacher ratio is lowered, we know so much more can be accomplished. This teacher worked with only 13 students. He was able to see positive changes in them within a five-week period. Could this have been done with a class of 30 in the same time?

How could teaching time been used more effectively? The district, first of all, should have placed the students in the appropriate bilingual classrooms. If proper placement was not possible, the teachers should have been given the time, the structure, and the opportunity to develop a plan for the successful integration of these two bilingual student groups.

Perhaps both this teacher and the Chinese bilingual teacher could have utilized cooperative learning strategies in the regular classroom between the Latino and Chinese students. If a sharing of cultures and languages among the students occurred, the Latino students' feelings of resentment, anger, and favoritism could possibly have been prevented. All students could have been encouraged to value and understand each other's cultural diversity and to respect each other's traditions, customs, and languages.

From the very beginning, this teacher and his students could have collaboratively brainstormed suggestions that would help the students to learn. Clear and firm expectations should have been established.

In order to encourage his students to speak Spanish, the teacher could have made a consistent effort to utilize the native language both in his teaching and in his personal contact with these students. When he called his students on the phone in the evenings just to talk, did he speak Spanish? During classroom lessons and activities, did he teach almost entirely in Spanish? If he had, his students would have followed his lead.

This teacher might have used district resource staff, as well as volunteers, to work in small groups or on a one-to-one basis. He might have asked native Spanish role models to speak to the students or provide demonstrations in the classroom. These activities would have engaged students in proactive learning and interaction with each other.

Instead of "watering down" the curriculum by providing unchallenging assignments, the teacher could have had students participate in plays, skits, music, and dance integrated with literature, science, math, etc. — all incorporating the Spanish language. Activities such as these would provide exciting, innovative, literature-based curriculum while facilitating Spanish and helping students achieve success.

As educators, we can only make assumptions as to why this situation occurred and about the progress of these students. We do know that these students were loved and understood because the teacher cared, respected, and valued their self-worth. These students were beginning to raise their self-esteem and feel happy about themselves. Can we conclude this teacher made a positive impact and difference in these students' lives? Did the relationship between this teacher and his students become even stronger as more bonding and teamwork developed? We can only feel it did.

Case 10

From "Outsider" to Active Learner: Struggles in a Newcomer School

This story of a boy named Mario illustrates the complexities I have encountered over many years of teaching in an inner-city elementary newcomer center where children need much support. It happened in my second year of teaching when I was still finding my way in this unique school. Everything seemed urgent then, and we weren't getting a lot of district guidance. I was frustrated because I wanted to provide the best education for my students.

I was born in this country to new immigrant parents from Mexico. In the early years, I can remember my parents struggling to make ends meet. Yet their primary goal was to provide educational opportunities that would make our lives easier. I was lucky enough to get a four-year scholarship to study at a major university in Mexico. It was there that I became highly politicized and decided to return to the United States in 1974 to participate in the Chicano movement. Since then, I have focused my energies on issues of immigrant rights, especially on providing educational opportunities for their children. Thus it is not surprising that I have spent 10 years teaching at this newcomer school.

Our student population is 100 percent Hispanic, and all students are newly arrived immigrants. Some come to escape civil war; many to flee poverty. Most come from rural or small provincial areas. They study here for one academic year, then usually transfer to bilingual programs throughout the district. The primary educational goal is to upgrade their academic skills in their native Spanish and to teach English as a second language. We teach the core curriculum in Spanish throughout the year.

During the first week of school that year, the principal walked into my third grade classroom with Mario. I immediately recognized him from the previous year; he was constantly being punished in the yard. The principal told me that Mario was being retained in third grade because he could not read in Spanish, much less in English. In general, his skills were very low, and he had

serious discipline problems. She thought he would do well with me because I have good management skills and am a strict teacher.

My initial reaction was anger. I felt I was being penalized. I already had 27 students, and at least five were non-readers. Having heard many negative comments about Mario from other teachers, I was also concerned that I might not like him. But here he was, and I needed to come up with a plan.

I decided on an approach that I felt would allow me to reach Mario, while at the same time keeping him from dominating the class. It's clear in retrospect that I was more concerned about Mario's behavior than his lack of skills. As I always do, I made every effort to create an attractive physical environment. Before school began, I had decorated the room with posters, charts and slogans, creating one or two "centers" and an area to display student work. All displays were selected to serve as *realia* to the themes that I base my instructional plans on. For example, I begin with the theme of "Who Am I," and derive lessons from students' personal experience. In October and November, we study indigenous cultures of Mexico and Central America to promote their Latino cultural heritage. As the themes change throughout the year, so do the displays. When appropriate, I make comparisons to U.S. and Latin American celebrations. I make every effort to encourage and allow students to feel that the classroom belongs to all of us.

On a daily basis during the first week of school, I go over the rules and classroom management procedures, such as the tasks for monitors and uses of equipment. Since Mario came mid-week, I thought it wise to firmly stress the rules and routines. I spent an hour explaining why we all had a responsibility to the group, why room maintenance is important, and what makes for a successful classroom.

In simple terms, I explained that we all have differences, but also common goals. We would try to share these goals in order to learn and be happy. I told them my expectations: I wanted cooperation, a hard-work ethic, active self-expression, and everyone participating in all facets of the class and striving for his or her best. I also needed order and quiet at appropriate times.

I then asked the children to help set our classroom standards by sharing their ideas. They responded by saying they would study hard, behave well, and respect the teacher. This last part, I knew, reflected the traditional Latin American attitude of pleasing those in authority. Children are taught to obey and respect adults, especially teachers, whether they're right or wrong. Poor people are treated in a patronizing manner, which results in a subservient structure. I do everything possible to break this pattern while still retaining the warmth and respectful customs of our culture. I teach children to feel secure in their ideas and opinions.

Mario, I think, liked this interaction. He seemed to be observing and, more importantly, understanding. He heard his peers expressing themselves in such cheerful, respectful and positive ways. This was all new to him, especially since he had been in a poorly managed classroom the previous year. He needed to get the message that this was a good group and he could be a part of it.

After a few days I decided to have a private talk with him. I told him I was very concerned that he had not learned to read. And I said I had heard about his behavior problems. In my class, I told him, everyone is expected to be their best and contribute to the well-being of the group. I would not tolerate rudeness, disruptions or laziness. I made it clear that I frequently called, wrote to and met with parents.

At the time, I thought that a "get tough" approach was needed to scare Mario into cooperating. But he quickly proved me wrong; he wasn't a lot of trouble. He caused only the minor disruptions of a rascal, doing silly things like pulling someone's hair or talking too much. Usually these things occurred when he could not read like his peers or could not do the assignment. I know his behavior reflected his insecurity and low self-esteem.

Every day for the first two months we discussed our rules and routines. I thought it important, especially for Mario. It appeared he needed help focusing on individual goals in order to succeed. He did not have a clear idea why he was in school. Perhaps he was doubtful of the rewards. Many disadvantaged people do not see education as a way to make their lives change because the rewards in a depressed area are limited. I had to help Mario understand why learning to read was more than just pleasing the teacher.

One problem that did annoy me was Mario's frequent failure to do his homework. I would keep him in at recess to make up the work, but he would be so sloppy about it that I would fume. When I told him how I felt, he would promise to do better. I knew his reading skills were improving, but he could do so much more. I wrote many notes to his parents. Frustratingly, even if they signed them, they would never call or write.

The turning point came when Mario and I got very mad at each other. I really scolded him in front of everybody. I said his work was careless and if he planned to continue this way he could go to another classroom, although I knew this probably was not possible. I insisted he tell his mother to come see me, no matter what she had to do to get here.

During recess he came to me with his head hanging low. He asked me to forgive him. His mother could not come, he said, because she had to work and was having lots of problems with his father. I could see that something was seriously wrong. I began asking about his home life. Mario, a tough little boy, began crying. He related that his father treated his mother, sister, and him terribly. My heart went out to him, and we both cried.

I wanted to rescue the entire family, most of all Mario. But how could I help? I told him that the best thing he could do was get the most out of school. "A person with knowledge can control his life and make things positive," I said. "You may not be able to change the situation at home, but you can make decisions that will directly help you." I promised to be there for him. For the rest of the day Mario was very quiet, and I felt introspective and sad.

Deep down, I think, Mario knew he was smart and could do well; he simply had to get past self-doubts. After our discussion he began changing. He accepted me as his friend and teacher. He did his homework and classwork and even began coming to school freshly bathed and wearing clean white shirts buttoned to the collar. I, of course, complimented him all the time. My husband and I bought him a light blue shirt, and I fondly recall the smile that put on his face.

One day Mario's mother finally came in — to thank me. Mario was not only doing well in school, but she said he was cooperating at home. He had described me to her as *brava* — tough, but good. She and I shared a laugh. We agreed to meet periodically or talk by phone. After that, she called me at home many times.

Mario really began to blossom. He got completely involved in classroom interactions. He dropped his "outsider" stance and became first an observer, then a participant, striving to do well academically. Actually, he had a major advantage over the other students. Besides being a thinker and problem solver, he was an excellent communicator. He shared opinions about everything and enjoyed knowing everybody else's business.

His abilities were evident in his reading progress. In Spanish he went from non-reader to third grade level by March and ended the year at fourth grade level. He had also begun reading English, using the ESL Reading Developmental Program.

Over the years I have wondered exactly what triggered Mario's desire to learn. How might I improve my teaching methods to help other students like him?

My major regret from that year is that I could not read out loud daily, since we had so few Spanish literature books. I am sure all the students would have achieved high academic levels if more literature would have been available. But I am pleased by my success with Mario. I think that three of my major beliefs affected him and all of my students, my aide, and myself. First, I believe that everyone can learn and achieve his or her goals. Second, strong self-esteem must be fostered in students. And third, an interesting classroom environment is essential — in my case, one that supports the Latino-oriented themes of my curriculum.

I often think about Mario. He came to my classroom as a low achiever; he left high in both achievement and confidence. Not every such student I have had turns around as spectacularly. But my experience with him is my model of the "whole student" approach I have tried to use since knowing him.

Sharon Nelson-Barber, Lecturer
Stanford University

This case is an interesting account of a bilingual teacher, herself a child of new immigrant parents, who strives to provide the best education for her own newly arrived immigrant students. Though not a "newcomer" to the United States herself, her varied experiences as a first generation Latina, a college student in Mexico, a participant in the Chicano movement, and finally as an educator, have engendered a special sensitivity to many of the obstacles her students face as they hone their skills and begin to learn English in preparation for transfer to regular bilingual classrooms. The case raises important questions about the ways in which teacher and students forge connections with one another, which I believe could be one of the most important elements in these students' progression out of the newcomer center.

The problem began when one more child was assigned to this teacher's class of 27 special needs students. And this was not just any other child, but a child known to have low abilities and "serious discipline problems" — a child who would need even more support. The teacher was "angry," and had every right to be.

This scenario, repeated in hundreds of classrooms across our nation, exemplifies the added demands placed on all of today's teachers as they try to sort out how best to serve children with special needs. Since teachers are inadequately trained to handle student diversity, they often turn to "local experts" — the African-American teacher who is effective with young male African-American students regarded by their other teachers as behavior problems; the Native-American teacher who engages native students in lengthy discussions in the classroom, though their other teachers say they are "reluctant," "quiet," or "shy"; or the white teacher who attends her students' *quinceañeras* and shops in the community or visits families on her way home, when other teachers leave quickly at the end of the day. These experts, who have struggled to "find [their] way,"

usually without "a lot of district guidance," discover their efforts leave them burdened with added responsibilities — more students, more meetings, less time to plan for their own classrooms. In addition, these teachers often are asked to serve on schoolwide committees or on local boards committed to school improvement.

As overextended as they may be, they may feel reluctant to turn down such invitations and lose voice in "making a difference." At the same time, they may feel resentful that the demands made on them are greater than on other teachers and question why other teachers aren't held accountable for knowing how to interact with diverse groups of learners. In addition to feeling "penalized," contend Montero-Sieburth and Perez (1987), bilingual teachers find that such experiences contribute to feelings of "marginality" in the profession — that their classes really are "waiting rooms" where students "stay until they are admitted to the mainstream" (p. 186-187). These authors go on to say that this often leads to a sense of isolation similar to that experienced by immigrant students.

Based on their year-and-a-half-long study of a Puerto Rican bilingual teacher of immigrant students, Montero-Sieburth and Perez (1987) offer additional insights into the particular challenges these teachers face.

> Such a teacher, aware of the dominant culture's requirements and sensitive, at the same time, to the immigrants' predicaments and aspirations, comes to play a crucial role in guiding the selection of elements in the dominant culture that are functional and essential, while helping the students to retain a necessary measure of self-respect through the preservation of their identity (p. 180).

In the context of this analysis of the immigrant experience, it seems Mario's teacher tackled her role's tasks with varying degrees of success.

Though the principal hailed her expertise with newcomer students, citing "good management skills" and a reputation as "a strict teacher," I would argue that this teacher's strengths go well beyond an ability to, as she says, "get tough" with kids. For example, she linked course content to students' life experiences, helped them maintain their identity using themes and activities that promote Latino cultural heritage, and discouraged the use of insulting references to "class" differences that are often a part of verbal sparring among Latinos. Still, due to the additional time and attention Mario required, she found she needed to devise even more strategies, which lent to her annoyance and frustration.

Admitting more concern for Mario's "behavior" than his "lack of skills," she decided to try not to overburden him with expectations, offering him instead a circumscribed, predictable set of rules and routines for behavioral success in her class. She did this keeping in mind that children who come to the United States to "escape civil war" or to "flee poverty" are "doubtful of the rewards" of education. With upheaval and uncertainty so much a part of their recent past, she was aware that these children need time to acquire more positive perspectives.

However, what she may not have had time to consider is that newcomers' isolation from family left behind, familiar surroundings, language, and in Mario's case, family problems, also leave them burdened with worries that can outweigh concern for school attendance, and often their studies. Perhaps Mario's "frequent failure to do his homework" or his tendency to be "sloppy" with his work were really indicators of his bewilderment with his new circumstances. Though aware that Mario's "behavior reflected his insecurity and low self-esteem," she may have been discouraged that all of her efforts "to encourage and allow students to feel that the classroom belongs to all of us" were not necessarily working for him.

The turning point came when Mario's teacher learned that "something was seriously wrong" at home. During their emotional discussion, "[her] heart went out to him, and [they] both cried." This expression of genuine emotion on the part of the teacher may have been the most "human" interaction Mario had experienced since he entered school. It was honest and "real," not guarded and distanced. It seems he could now believe that this teacher really cared.

Though emotion can be viewed as counterproductive to the teaching role (Duke & Mechkel, 1984; Kochman, 1981), various ethnic groups place a great deal of value on teachers' displays of emotion (Delpit & Nelson-Barber, forthcoming). The notion of "caring," brought to the nation's attention by Jaime Escalante in the movie *Stand and Deliver*, is a common theme discussed among teachers of Latino students. A colleague from Columbia University, Maria Torres-Guzman, names at least three concepts — *respeto, cariño,* and *ganas* — that form important bases for engagement with students and play an important role in their schooling success. She explains that these concepts embody many emotions; mutual respect, caring, loving relationships with students, enthusiasm, expectation, guts, desire, courage, and determination to win against all odds and against one's personal weaknesses, etc. It is motivating forces such as these that allow students to view their classrooms as communities founded on equality and mutual respect and ones in which they do not have to give up their individuality for the sake of an education.

With current projections showing that in the next five years Latino school populations will increase more rapidly than any other group in the United States (Morganthau, 1990), all teachers would do well to consider how they will go about developing personal bonds with students if they are to help them learn to function within the fabric of mainstream life and overcome what Montero-Sieburth and Perez (1987) term "the vicious cycle of exclusion, poverty, and demoralization" (p.183).

Given the current trend toward reflectiveness in teaching, it is clear that special needs teachers like Mario's had to learn to be reflective long ago.

REFERENCES

Delpit, L., & Nelson-Barber, S. (forthcoming). Rethinking issues of context and culture for the new teacher. *Anthropology & Education Quarterly*.

Duke, D., & Mechkel, A. (1984). *Teachers' guide to classroom management*. New York: Random House.

Kochman, T. (1981). *Black and white styles in conflict*. Chicago: University of Chicago Press.

Montero-Sieburth, M., & Perez, M. (1987). Echar pa'lante, Moving onward: The dilemmas and strategies of a bilingual teacher. *Anthropology & Education Quarterly, 18*, 180-189.

Morganthau, T. (Fall/Winter, 1990). The future is now, Education: A consumer's handbook. *Newsweek* (special issue), pp. 72-76.

Michi Pringle, Staff Developer
San Francisco Unified School District

I am in agreement with this teacher's three major beliefs — they are effective for all students, but critical for newcomer students as we strive to equip them for success in their new country. Education is seen as the key to success by many immigrant groups. The low-income level of so many Latinos nationwide is directly tied to low educational levels. At the newcomer center we have a "window" to reach students and families when they are most receptive to suggestions that can lead to continuing school success.

This teacher was very effective because she made Mario — previously treated as an outcast — feel like part of the group. She also let him (and the other students) see her as a person, not just a teacher. All her students know she cares deeply about them, and that personal connection is very important to our immigrant children. She feels passionately about the value of education and holds high expectations for all her students. They respond to that.

The dilemma of a newcomer center is how to ameliorate conflicts arising from differences between the home culture and mainstream/school culture. We need to be aware of which Latino characteristics may be misinterpreted or have maladaptive consequences for children as they enter the U.S. mainstream. For example, Latinos and immigrants from other cultures are raised to defer to authority. Teachers may like that because the students are more manageable; but it works to the students' detriment because they don't learn to stand up for themselves — a trait valued in this country. Students being reprimanded by a teacher will look down or away, as though they're not paying attention. But in their culture, looking the teacher in the eye would be considered defiant. Latino children are taught that it is "prideful" to call attention to themselves as individuals; the U.S. mainstream admires the "tooting of your own horn." When the children allow others to speak for them ("Ana's pencil broke, she needs to use the pencil sharpener" or "Jorge needs another piece of paper"), teachers may interpret the behavior as timidity or "passivity." But as we educate children to become more "Americanized" it is important to educate their parents as well, so as not to aggravate intergenerational conflicts when children start acting "disrespectful" at home with their "American ways."

The mission of the newcomer center is to set the student on the road to becoming truly bicultural and bilingual, able to function and participate fully in two cultures and to take pride in being able to identify with both cultures. To achieve this goal, we build on the strengths the children bring from their mother culture and develop other characteristics valued by mainstream society in this country.

Our Latino children come from homes that value cooperation; everyone works for the good of the family, not for individual fame/gain. Understanding this, teachers can plan appropriate activities for educating these youngsters to live in a society that values the individual above the group. Correctly implemented, cooperative learning strategies result in mastery in academic skill areas, while also validating social attitudes the children already have toward working together, thus enhancing self esteem. Implementation of Teacher Expectation and Student Achievement (TESA) interactions supports students in their development from dependent to more independent, self-reliant learners.

The charge of the newcomer center is to find a balance between our academic hopes for the children, preparing them for success in mainstream society, and understanding/supporting the family values and dynamics from their home culture. We do not want to damage the family unit — a great strength of the Latin culture. We do not want to emphasize only the cognitive realm at the expense of the affective. A student who succeeds academically does better with support from the home.

Many come from rural backgrounds, from isolated ranches and small villages. A large city such as San Francisco is completely alien to them. Accustomed to having little or no voice in their home countries, these people are unlikely to assert themselves here, particularly if they are undocumented. Their attitude is that the teachers are the professionals when it comes to educating their children; it should be left to them, without interference/input from parents. The few parents coming from a middle class background are much more sophisticated; they know what they can demand for their children and how to work the system.

We work to help parents be aware of some of the pitfalls and to support them in their adaptation to this country. We refer them to language classes and health/counseling services, offer workshops on what they can do at home to foster school-readiness skills, to encourage their children's growing self-assertiveness, and to maintain two-way communication with their children. We offer insights into cultural differences and describe the peer pressure their children will encounter after leaving the Center. We define their rights as parents to demand a quality education for their children and their responsibility to participate in and monitor the educational system. By helping parents, we help kids. And hopefully, down the line, we avoid or ameliorate some problems.

Schools often find themselves unable to bridge socioeconomic, linguistic, and cultural differences with students' homes. Experienced teachers know that teacher and school are somewhat like a second family, working — ideally — with the first family to increase the child's learning. But the difficulties of disenfranchisement, busing, limited-English proficiency, and differing cultural perceptions of teachers and schools have become obstacles to effectively linking the two worlds.

Families caught in cycles of poverty and school failure often do not see education as a source of hope or well-being. When teachers and administrators don't understand and don't work to bridge racial and cultural differences, parent and child may have no way to develop a sense of identity with the school. In the extreme, some members of the disenfranchised community may come to openly distrust the school as a supportive environment for their children. Meanwhile, the family values of many immigrant newcomers may discourage parents from being candid or assertive with school staff. In Asia and Latin America, educators enjoy high status and authority. Parents accustomed to deferring to teachers find it difficult to adopt North America's give-and-take exchange. Parent-teacher relations are also affected by cultural parenting styles, immigration trauma, or other psychological problems, and even gender role conflicts experienced by some newcomer families.

CHAPTER 4

The Influence of Parents and Community

The three cases presented here deal with very distinct instances of parent involvement. In **My "Good Year" Explodes: A Confrontation With Parents**, a teacher's career and reputation are threatened when active parents express dissatisfaction with her performance. Parents in this case are intensely involved in school decision-making. Conflicts arise over modes of communication, cultural values, and disparate educational goals. Accompanying commentaries offer intriguingly different ways to perceive each party's actions.

Opening Pandora's Box: The Mystery Behind an "Ideal Student" is perhaps one of the most haunting cases in the book because it unravels a mystery, only to reveal a poignant dilemma for a child, a teacher, and a family. The teacher's candid description of her relationship with Connie illuminates how deeply such factors as cultural styles, gender roles, and family discord can affect the learning situation. Along with the teacher, we are troubled by the unspoken tensions in Connie's Chinese family. The commentaries help guide us in sensitively pondering the teacher's actions and the family's behavior.

In **Home Visits** we encounter a teacher who risks entering the tense and sometimes hostile communities where her students live in order to gain mutual understanding and cooperation with their extended families. New perceptions and insights on both sides prove a boon to student learning.

Case 11

My "Good Year" Explodes: A Confrontation With Parents

I thought it had been a good year. My second grade class of 32 bilingual students was a joy to teach. Like me, a third of my students were Japanese immigrants. Another third were Japanese Americans who were born in the United States, and the rest were from a mix of ethnic backgrounds. The entire class had progressed in math, according to their scores on the California Test of Basic Skills. With three weeks left of the school year, I was confident that I had covered all the math strands from the California State Framework. Moreover, because of strong parent involvement and participation, we had enjoyed a variety of enrichment activities such as art, music, dance, and other performing arts.

Early one spring morning as I prepared for class, Grace — the PTA president — walked in. Grace was a Caucasian parent and a regular volunteer in my classroom. With just five minutes to class time, she handed me a letter and said, "Don't read this now because it will make you unhappy. Wait until after school."

My puzzled look prompted her to say more. "Some parents felt you could have done a better job teaching our children. Do you think you really did a good job this year?"

I couldn't believe what I was hearing. The bell rang, but I ignored it and opened the letter. As I read, tears filled my eyes. I was too shaken to begin class. Instead, I went straight to my principal, Mr. Bryant.

Grace followed me in. Mr. Bryant seemed to be expecting me; he had been given a copy of the letter. "You may leave," he said to Grace, who was by now in tears herself. "We didn't mean to hurt you," she said to me. "We wanted you to know how we felt."

When Grace was gone, Mr. Bryant gave me a hug, offered me tea, and sent another teacher to cover my class. As I regained my composure, we discussed the letter. I learned that copies signed by parents had been sent to the principal, the district office, and the school board. Apparently, the letter had been triggered by the news that I would be teaching a combination class next year. When parents realized that I might be teaching their children again, they decided to express their concern that I had inappropriately taught the basic concepts, particularly in math.

The children had been allowed to explore and learn with manipulatives. Parents felt that they hadn't brought home enough paper and pencil homework and math worksheets. They also thought that if their children were in my class next year, they would not progress at the rate of other students. They apparently wanted their children to spend their math time on rote memorization, drill and practice, and traditional tasks.

My mind raced back to a visit I'd had with one of the mothers early in the year. She had come to me holding a stack of ditto sheets that her daughter had completed in first grade. "Look how much more she was learning last year," the mother had said.

I had explained to her my firm belief that my hands-on approach and problem-solving strategies were far more effective for all my students than traditional "drill and skill" methods. I told her that I used the mandated California State Mathematics Framework and that I had attended numerous workshops and training programs to learn how to incorporate these techniques into my teaching. The children, I pointed out, felt challenged and were highly motivated to learn math as a result. The mother had listened intently, and I thought she heard my message.

On Back-to-School night, I had carefully explained my strategies to all the parents. Throughout the school year I also kept a running communication about all curriculum, special projects, and student progress and concerns through letters, telephone calls, and weekly student checklists. Parents had numerous opportunities to contact me, but no one ever did.

Our school has always encouraged active parent participation. My classroom was no exception. The parents who seemed unhappy with my math curriculum helped regularly in my classroom. They saw me teach hands-on, integrated math lessons and they watched their children engage in critical thinking and problem-solving activities. To reinforce skills with limited English proficient students, I often used concrete materials, visuals, sheltered English techniques, or — when I could — the child's primary language. Never did I feel that my teaching abilities were in doubt.

In the days that followed my talk with Mr. Bryant, I also conferred with other teachers, the principal, other administrators, and even professors. I wanted to know what they thought, but most of all I needed emotional support. My pride and dignity had been wounded when my professionalism and integrity were questioned. Worse, I had been accused of doing a disservice to the children. I was haunted by thoughts that I had brought this on myself, and I was full of guilt.

The network of colleagues supported me. They felt that the parents' actions reflected not a failure of mine with the children, but a lack of parent acceptance of new teaching strategies. They bolstered me with reminders that I had been selected as a mentor teacher and my work was regarded as outstanding.

But I am still puzzled. Why did parents think that their children would have different experiences in other teachers' classrooms? Each school year we address the various curriculum areas in many parent education workshops taught by mentor teachers, administrators, and specialists in the curriculum development areas. My teaching approaches are not different from those of the majority of teachers at my school. We share philosophies and use similar techniques.

Was it a personality conflict between the parents — such as Grace — and me? Was it a cultural problem, rooted in differing communication styles, learning expectations, or traditions? Why couldn't parents come directly to me when concerns first arose? Did they feel they should have had more control over what happened in the classroom? What was the true catalyst for their action?

Since this incident, our staff has had many collegial meetings to brainstorm ways of averting such problems in the future. A schoolwide grievance committee has been established, composed of the administrator, paraprofessionals, teachers, and parents. We have also established a procedure for communications. Parents must meet with the teacher first. If issues remain unresolved, all parties meet with the administrator. The final recourse is the executive parent body.

But I often still ask myself how I missed seeing warning signs. I have always put much effort into my work. It was terribly disturbing to face this quandary at the end of school. I was ready to quit the very profession I loved and to which I have dedicated years of service. Did I cause these parents to react the way they did? What did I do wrong? What should I do in the future if parents and I disagree about how best to teach their children?

*Larry Cuban
Stanford University*

To this teacher, a complaint from a group of parents about her teaching of math clanged like an alarm bell in the still of the night. It jangled her nerves, upset her emotional balance, and led her to question whether she should remain a teacher — a powerful reaction from an experienced teacher. What appeared to me initially as an over-reaction became partially understandable as I began to think about the meaning this teacher attached to the letter from several parents.

The teacher believes in her heart and mind that she is providing the very best math instruction to a class of 32 bilingual students. Moreover, she has attended workshops to improve her teaching of the new state curricular guide. Finally, she had made good-faith efforts to keep parents informed of what she had done. In fact, because of strong parent involvement in the class, there have been more art, music, and other performing arts activities. Then, like a lightening bolt out of the blue comes a complaining letter from several parents. The very core of the teacher's self-concept as an experienced professional had been questioned by a group of parents whose warning signals she may have missed. Seen in this context, the teacher's shock may be interpreted as coming from someone whose very identity as a teacher had been challenged by several parents whose cultural background was similar to her own.

Note that placing this contextual underbrush around the incident makes the teacher's reaction partially understandable. To understand it better, I could speculate that this teacher had never before received a written complaint from parents, no less one delivered by the PTA president. Perhaps this is the first time the teacher faced a direct challenge to her teaching, and since the complaint came from the PTA president and went directly to the principal, it was humiliating. The teacher's shock may be due to her unfamiliarity with being the target of parent complaints, being confronted about her teaching, or dealing with open conflict.

Some perspective may help. While it is uncommon for non-English speaking parents to complain to a teacher and school, it is not unheard of either in inner-city schools or suburbs. There are instances of ethnic parents complaining to school authorities about what happened in classrooms their children attended. In New York City just before World War I, for example, poor immigrant parents from Eastern Europe protested a new system of schooling called the Gary Plan (after Gary, Indiana) because it meant that academic class time would be decreased for their children. German parents in mid-19th century St. Louis hounded school officials to teach German in the schools. In the South during and after the civil rights movement, many black parents challenged both teachers and administrators about what happened in classrooms.

Similarly, parental complaints in suburbs are routine, where parents visit classrooms to shop for those teachers best matched to their children. Teachers and principals in affluent towns are intimately familiar with giving detailed explanations to parents about the latest state-approved textbook, the new family-life curriculum, and why the sixth grade teachers don't team like they do in the other elementary schools.

Fortunately, the damage done to the teacher's self-esteem was partially alleviated by the principal and colleagues, who rallied around her in the days following the incident. In trying to understand what happened to her, it may be helpful to lay out what the teacher defined as the problem and what solutions she and the school arrived at to prevent recurrences of such an event.

The teacher is puzzled by the parents' complaint. She poses alternative ways of framing the problem: Were parents unaware that other teachers in this school taught in a similar fashion? Was there a personality conflict between her and particular parents? Were there cultural differences "rooted in differing communication styles, learning expectations, or traditions"? Did parents want more control over how the teacher taught? She doesn't answer these well-put queries. Given the information presented, it is difficult to determine which of these framings of the problem are the strongest candidates. Note, however, that she chose to frame each problem differently, thus suggesting very different directions to travel in solving each.

I then looked at how the teacher and school handled the conflict. The solutions the school adopted and implemented had nothing to do with how the teacher framed the problem. A schoolwide grievance committee was established that included a parent. As part of the procedure, a new rule was laid down: parents must meet with the teacher first if there is a complaint. If no satisfaction is obtained, then both parties meet with the principal. The final appeal is to the executive parent body. This bureaucratic solution has little to do with what the puzzled teacher posed as alternatives.

The school-devised solution is familiar, even though it may well be inappropriate — particularly if there were cultural barriers to communicating with parents about classroom activities. The complaint and the way that it was channeled through the PTA president suggests to me cultural issues around what constitutes a "good" math activity in class and a desire to avoid open conflict with an authority such as a teacher, who is highly respected in Asian cultures. The usual ways that a teacher and school tell culturally diverse parents what their children are learning and how they learn it often fail to convey what is intended. Though it's admirable that the school and teacher hold meetings and send out newsletters, it doesn't necessarily follow that parents from particular groups either understand or agree with what the school is doing. Different cultural beliefs about proper ways of teaching and handling conflict are subtle and important. In this situation, such beliefs bear further examination before being ruled out as the source of the conflict between the teacher and the complaining

parents. I raise the possibility of lapses in cross-cultural communication because the bureaucratic solution arrived at by the school community could squelch rather than encourage parent input about what is appropriate for their children.

I felt the pain that this teacher expressed. She appears well-intentioned, hard-working, and dedicated to doing the best job that she can with a large class of bilingual children. She felt that her integrity as a teacher was challenged. Given the limited information presented, however, I interpreted her description of what happened as laying implicit blame upon parents for not being more understanding of how hard she, the teacher, worked. In doing so, the teacher, I believe, missed the larger issue of miscues in cultural communication. To her credit, she noted this possibility. I wished she had pursued it.

Diane Garfield, Teacher
San Francisco Unified School District

As a member of the staff and close colleague of this outstanding teacher, I was deeply disturbed by the situation. Because I teach in the same hands-on manner at the same school with the same active and vocal parents, I also felt attacked. It was interesting that we all felt as personally affected as the teacher involved.

The situation made us feel vulnerable to attack. Our integrity was on the line. At stake were not only the positive relationships we thought we had with the parents, but our innovative teaching methods and even our philosophy of education. Why was this exemplary teacher singled out? Even after time, that question remains unanswered. There are some positive things that have come of this, however. As a result of several faculty meetings — stimulated by the incident — we are now a unified staff with a stated and written process for complaints, and we are more clear than ever about our teaching objectives.

Until this point we had been rather loose in the way we managed our relationships with the parents. We were always able to handle the day-to-day problems as they arose. But we learned that it was necessary to develop a standardized grievance policy to deal with potential problems. Now all problems must be discussed with the teacher first. If that is unsatisfactory, the parents can appeal to a teacher committee and then to the principal. This feels good; we truly feel empowered. With this ground to stand on, it will not be nearly as easy for parents to come forth and puncture our souls.

Possibly the parents scared themselves a little. They were becoming ever more powerful and vocal, when suddenly they went too far. Of course, as in any situation of this kind, only a few were the culprits — the rest were totally in the dark and, when informed, disapproved of the other parents' actions. I believe this situation helped the less vocal and more supportive members of the community come forward. Many of those who caused the pain are no longer active in the community.

Parents are an important component at our school. They help raise considerable monies to support our innovative programs. Yet, it has now become clear to our educational community that it is the teachers along with the administration who will determine educational policy, not the parents. We welcome parent support, their participation, and the interest they show in their children's education, but we are the professionals, and we set the educational policy for our classrooms.

We now have a firm process for dealing with situations should they occur. We are a tightly knit group. We have left our classrooms to become good friends who now support one another on a daily basis, not just in crisis. It is unfortunate that it took such a negative scenario to lead our school a step closer to the excellence for which we continually strive.

Carne Barnett, Mathematics Educator
Far West Laboratory

It is easy to dismiss the concern of these parents as culturally motivated. After all, the stereotype of Asian parents is that they value regimented drill and copious homework for their children, rather than an activity-based math program. While I am inclined to believe that the teacher in this situation is competently implementing a strong and innovative mathematics program in her classroom, we should not overlook the possibility that the parents could have a legitimate concern. Teachers are increasingly aware of a national movement in mathematics education that deemphasizes rote drill and practice and puts a stronger emphasis on thinking and understanding. They are becoming enthusiastic about having their students use manipulatives, do problem solving, and have fun with mathematical games and activities. But it is possible for children to *use* manipulatives, *do* problem solving, and *have fun* with mathematical games and activities without greatly enhancing their understanding of mathematics.

Manipulatives, for example, can be just as abstract as mathematical symbols if links are not made to a child's experience and to other mathematical ideas that a child already knows. A non-investigative approach to problem solving can result in learners who search for a rule rather than apply thinking and reasoning strategies. Likewise, math games and activities can be enjoyed by students who do not know their purpose or place in the larger mathematical picture. It could be that the parents, even those who agree in principle with the teacher's goals, feel that their youngsters are not developing a cohesive or thorough understanding of math. As teachers we must constantly assess what our students are learning and how they are integrating that knowledge into something that makes sense to them. Upon reflection, even very well-intentioned teachers may realize that they have a lot to learn when it comes to putting innovative approaches into practice.

Christine W. Hiroshima, Staff Developer
San Francisco Unified School District

In reading this case, I was struck by the cultural implications — not so much between the teacher and the students, but between the teacher and the parents. The cultural dissonance here is complicated. This class is in a primarily monocultural bilingual school comprising mostly Asian students, half of them immigrants. But the complaint issued to the teacher was delivered by a Caucasian parent. The majority of parents of this school population are, in fact, Asian.

I am really surprised at the action taken by these parents. I realize that parents unfamiliar to the United States' school system would have difficulty understanding goals of instruction that this faculty is trying to implement. They are probably much more used to a system where pencil and paper tasks are equated with education. However, while it is probably safe to assume that newly-arrived parents may indeed be less familiar with American schools, curriculum, instructional strategies, and methodologies, I wonder how this situation could escalate to the point where there is an impasse between the teacher and the parents. I find it very surprising that this particular group of parents (primarily recent immigrants and Asian-Americans), on their own, would confront the teacher with a letter expressing discontent with her professional integrity. I would venture to guess that, if those parents were unhappy with the way things were going in the classroom, they would have individually spoken to the principal about having their child removed from the class the following year. That would save embarrassment on the part of both the teacher and parents. A letter of discontent would be presumptuous and disrespectful and would cause the teacher to "lose face." I believe that if the leadership came from the Asian parents, the teacher would have been aware, however subtly, of their discontent; she would not have been shocked by the parents' action. Could it be that the Caucasian parent who delivered the letter somehow instigated the situation to this escalated level?

Perhaps the root of this case study encompasses a much broader perspective than the situation in this classroom. I am familiar with the school we are discussing, and I know that a large component of its success is due to the very active participation of the parents. In this era where effective schools research advocates for heavy parent involvement, issues surrounding that involvement are sometimes overlooked. In this particular school, parent involvement includes quite a bit of fundraising — for specific programs, for supplemental materials, even for support staff (paraprofessionals). If the parents have literally invested so much in their child's education, where does the school draw the line in determining how those funds are used? How do you deal with the conflicts arising out of the will of parents vs. the professional judgment of the faculty? How do you reconcile opposing perceptions of education when one side is funding the other?

The parents' perceptions of what *should* be happening may be incongruent with the classroom reality. However, it appears that the teacher informed them about classroom strategies and expectations. Not only do those strategies seem to be consistent with most other classrooms at the school, but channels for communication were in place and opportunities to discuss concerns were plentiful. The fundamental issues concerning the students themselves are not clear, and more information is needed to more fully assess the situation.

Beverly Jimenez, Consulting Principal
San Francisco Unified School District

I was asked to write this piece in late June. I am first sitting down to the task in October. It has taken this long for me to gain the perspective needed to thoughtfully respond. For me, the issues raised by this teacher reflect a nationwide lack of confidence in public school education. The wrenching ethical, economic, and institutional changes taking place in our society require that schools develop skills and abilities in students that may be very different from those familiar to their parents.

Ironically, this incident occurred at one of San Francisco's finest schools, a school where an extraordinarily committed certificated staff has spent countless unpaid hours collegially honing their professional skills and developing cutting-edge curricular content and instructional delivery strategies. Parents founded the school and have traditionally been integral to the decision-making processes regarding all aspects of school life.

Parents choose this particular school program for their child based on general and specific reputation, the opportunity for bilingual/bicultural education and family connection to the city's Asian community, test scores and other indicators of student achievement, the learning and play yard environments, the physical plant and location, and the climate and culture of parent participation in decision-making. To get their child placed in the school, parents spend the greater part of a year enmeshed in a frighteningly impersonal struggle with the procedures and restrictions that have been developed over the last two decades of court-ordered desegregation to ensure educational equity for all San Francisco public school students. To say the least, this experience does not engender trust, respect, or partnership between school people and parents. Despite considerable effort by school staff and parent committee members to keep communication open, a spontaneous external network of parents forms. Long after the struggle for placement is over, parents continue to rely on this network for information on whether the school will "deliver the goods" on their high expectations.

Once their child is in the school of choice, parents begin to lobby for their teacher of choice. This remains a critical "survival issue" through all the elementary school grades.

Teacher reputations created within the informal parent network are based on a myriad of criteria, including: personality, interactive abilities, years of experience, teaching philosophy and related style, student achievement, classroom climate and discipline, information flow, specific incidents, and paraprofessional relationships. These reputations do not remain static; they are subject to dramatic and sometimes catastrophic revision at any moment based on the players involved. The circumstances surrounding the creation of teacher reputation are further complicated by judgments stemming from the cultural diversity, conflicting cultural norms, and resultant expectations of the parent population itself. There is further perceptual division along cultural/generational lines, among parents with several children in the system, and among the increasing number who have only one child to invest with concern and protection. Within this atmosphere, it is the rare parent and teacher who create deep bonds of trust and partnership regarding a child's education.

The inherent tension between the parents' desire for the best schooling for their individual child and the school professional's attempt to create the most nurturing, challenging and coherent program for all its students is also at play in this most tenuous of relationships. A school that is responding to the changing needs of our students and society needs to be a dynamic community of learners. A collegial school climate and culture of safety for professional staff to experiment and take risk as they develop their skills is critically important; yet this climate must be created within the broader climate of mistrust for public education which permeates our society.

Asian cultural norms of respect for the classroom teacher and concerns for "face" couple with more generalized parental fears about negatively affecting a teacher's attitude toward their child. Parents become reluctant to confront teachers with fears and concerns throughout the school year, even though there are many established invitations to do so. Many parents require the safety of numbers, and/or a perceived major threat to their child's well-being, to openly bring up problems. At this point the amount of pent-up emotion and justification often prevents the problem-solving dialogue that would allow resolution of concern. The principal's consensus-making skills are challenged to the hilt; teachers justifiably feel attacked and seek their colleagues' support; the formal parent group leadership takes a stand. The solution process becomes painful and costly. And the result is a compromise that leaves all participants shaken.

How in truth are we to answer the questions raised by the teacher who wrote this case? I hope my perspective — which has been two years in the making — helps our dedicated professionals to see that they have not created the problem. Through their dedication and willingness to examine their own actions, they will continue to contribute to the climate of trust-building and partnership that needs to be created if we are to work together to prepare our children to be the well-educated, problem-solving adults they will need to be.

Opening
Pandora's Box:
The Mystery
Behind an "Ideal
Student"

The summer I changed schools and was unpacking in my new classroom, I suddenly noticed a very thin Asian girl with shoulder-length hair peeking in. She looked as if she were about to run away, so I said hello and invited her to join me. "Are you the new third grade teacher?" she whispered. When I said yes, she shyly looked down and said, "I'm going to be in your class." She didn't make a move to go so I began asking her questions. Her name, she said, was Connie. Born in Hong Kong, she had come to the United States when she was three. She had one brother who was going into first grade. Connie spent from 7:30 a.m. to 5:30 p.m. at the childcare center on the school site since both her parents worked. In addition, she attended Chinese school three days a week, which was taught on site. She spoke Chinese at home and had been to Hong Kong three times to visit relatives.

When school started, Connie proved to be an ideal student. She was cooperative, self-disciplined, motivated, artistic, and above grade level in every area. She loved to help and would often appear in my classroom after school. Given a choice, Connie preferred to work alone. However, she worked well in groups or in paired projects.

Her parents did not come to Back-to-School Night, and I told Connie I was eager to meet them. I met her father very briefly one evening when Connie brought him down to the classroom to introduce me. He appeared to be in a hurry and left quickly. The same thing occurred with her mother about a week later.

I began to notice that Connie would often play with a classmate named Mai Ling. If not with Mai Ling, she would usually be alone. She always asked to stay in at recess to help, and I often allowed her this.

All went well until October. I change seats randomly on the first school day of every month, and by chance Connie and Mai Ling were seated together for October. Everything seemed fine. I noticed that Connie would often bring things to Mai Ling in the morning — letters, origami, and other handmade paper things. Connie

would also bring these kinds of things to me. Then one day another student told me Connie was crying. Connie had her head down, and Mai Ling was as physically apart from her as possible at the table. This behavior continued off and on for about two weeks. Any attempts I made at talking to the girls either individually or together were fruitless. Both would withdraw or cry, but would not talk.

Seat changing time came again and the two girls were no longer together. They were no longer playing together as far as I knew. One morning I saw Connie give Mai Ling a letter. I asked Connie how things were going. She started to cry and I noticed she would bite her lower lip continuously as I talked to her. She told me Mai Ling would not be her friend and would not even talk to her.

The tears had escalated, so I decided to speak with the principal. When I explained my difficulty getting a response, she volunteered to speak with the girls. I carefully explained to Connie and Mai Ling that the principal was trying to help solve the problems they were having. She spoke to them at the end of the school day. When they left school, both looked very unhappy. The principal, I learned, had been unable to get much response from either girl. About an hour after school, Mai Ling's mother called me to find out what was happening. Mai Ling's sister had called her at work, saying that Mai Ling was in tears. She thought she was in serious trouble because she had been sent to the principal.

Mai Ling's mother explained that it was difficult to get Mai Ling to express her feelings. She would withdraw at home in the same way she would withdraw at school. I explained the situation with Connie, and Mai Ling's mother said she would make every attempt to talk with Mai Ling and let me know if she could supply any more information. The following day she called back. Between coaxing Mai Ling and talking with her sister, she had gathered that Connie wanted Mai Ling to be her best friend and not play with anyone else. Mai Ling liked to play with Connie, but she also wanted to play with other girls. When Mai Ling played with other friends, Connie would cry and go off by herself.

The following week was parent conferencing time. Mai Ling and Connie seemed friendly again. In my conference with Mai Ling's mother, I reported that all seemed to be going smoothly again. By chance, a new student arrived one morning before school had begun, and Connie was helping me in the classroom. I felt this might be a good opportunity for Connie to make a new friendship. I introduced the two girls and asked Connie if she would sit next to Annie and show her the routines. She moved her things, and then the bell rang. I brought my class up to the room and when I looked over to Connie and Annie, Connie had her back to Annie and was as far away from her as she could possibly be without being at the next table. I went over to see what was happening and overheard Connie say to another student in a very angry voice with her arms folded tightly across her body, "Ms. Johnson made me move over here." Annie was looking quite bewildered so I took Connie aside and asked her quietly if she wanted to go back to her old seat. She nodded her head. She moved back, and I asked for volunteers to sit at Annie's table. Every other girl in the class and a few boys raised their hands. I spoke with Connie at recess and tried to explain to her how a new student would feel. She bit her lip continuously and did not respond. She spent the rest of the day extremely sullen and withdrawn.

On Friday, Connie's mother came in for her conference. She mentioned the situation with Mai Ling immediately. Lowering her voice, she explained that she was very worried about Connie's friendship. She said Connie was obsessed with Mai Ling and it wasn't natural. She had intercepted a letter Connie had written expressing how much she liked Mai Ling and how unhappy she was that Mai Ling would not be her friend. She told me that Connie talked about Mai Ling constantly, wrote about her and made her gifts, and she was worried that this was not normal behavior for a third grade girl.

In fact, she kept repeating, "This is not normal." It seemed to me that she feared sexual implications, but I didn't pursue it. I explained to her what I had observed. When I asked if this had been a problem before, her response took me completely aback: Connie, she said, had threatened to cut her wrists when she was five years old because a friend wouldn't play with her anymore. "I really gave her a hard lesson that time," the mother went on. "I spanked her, and explained to her what suicide really means." A red flag went up in my mind.

Remaining composed, I described Connie's behavior with Annie that morning. Her mother was upset. At that point Connie happened to come into the room — she had a recess break from Chinese school. I invited her to join us, and explained what we were discussing. I told Connie I wasn't angry with her; I merely wanted her to understand how she had hurt another child's feelings. I asked her to think of how she would have felt in that situation. Connie began to bite her lip and not respond. Her mother said, "You have to make new friends." All of a sudden, Connie started crying. "I don't want new friends. I just want to be Mai Ling's friend."

You need more than one friend," said her mother.

Connie started to sob. "You gave away Sparky," she said. "He was my friend, and you didn't even tell me. You did it while I was in school."

While her mother interjected that the landlord wouldn't allow dogs, Connie kept on repeating, "You didn't even tell me you were going to do it." Sobbing and gasping for breath, she railed, "You never let me put anything on my bedroom walls. You always let Martin do what he wants to do, but you don't even let me talk on the telephone. Now you also stole my letters to Mai Ling!"

I was witnessing anger and resentment that I'd never seen before in Connie. She was crying uncontrollably. Her mother, on the other hand, seemed somewhat removed. She retorted each accusation calmly, soon mixing Chinese and English. Connie bit her lip continuously throughout this interchange.

To try to restore some calm, I gave Connie a hug and told her I hated to see her feeling so unhappy. I said that we needed to continue exploring these problems, but I felt that Connie was too upset to do so right then. I turned to addressing more positive matters and went over Connie's progress report with both of them, highlighting her academic achievements and skills. Not that this was necessarily the best course of action, but I didn't really know what else to do. I thought the situation called for professional counseling, but this surely didn't feel like the appropriate time to suggest this. I ended the conference very frustrated. I felt I had opened Pandora's Box.

All weekend I was distracted by what had occurred. I drafted a short memo to my principal suggesting that Connie may need professional counseling and asked her for a meeting to explain. I kept thinking about Connie's threatened attempt to cut her wrists at such an early age and about her mother's emotional remoteness.

When I related the situation to the principal early Monday morning, she seemed to feel that I had overreacted. But my gut level reaction was still one of deep concern.

I went to my classroom and found Connie there early. "I'm really sorry Ms. Johnson," she said. "I didn't mean to make you feel bad." This surprised me. Again I explained how I was concerned about her feelings. She told me her mother and father had talked with her for a long time over the weekend. They both wanted her to apologize to me. "But you don't owe me an apology," I said. Still she persisted in saying she was sorry for hurting my feelings. Somehow we were missing the real problem. I told Connie I was glad she had come in to see me and encouraged her to let me know if things weren't going well. About an hour after school started, Connie's father showed up. He said hello and asked if Connie had talked to me. When I said she had, he went over to her and gave her a kiss and hug. It was the first physical contact I had seen Connie receive from either parent. She seemed content and happy.

Since that day, I became extremely aware of Connie's behavior. There were some incidents — an unacknowledged birthday present to Mai Ling, a note from a substitute that said, "It appears that there is a long-term problem between Mai Ling and Connie," and some tears. One day in March, Connie burst into tears and explained that if she didn't have her times tables memorized by the weekend, she would get spanked by her father. I talked to her mother after school that evening and explained how Connie had just begun learning multiplication and had no problem with the concept. I also encouraged her to give Connie more time to memorize the tables and not to pressure her with a deadline. I assured her Connie had an excellent memory and would have no problem with memorization. I gave her suggestions and some materials for drill and practice and strongly advised against spanking. After that weekend, Connie returned to school in a much happier frame of mind, and it appeared that the pressure was off.

One day in April, Connie asked if she could talk with me privately. She told me she couldn't stop thinking about her dog, Sparky. She still missed him and couldn't get to sleep at night because she was so sad. She had hopes of getting him back. (Connie had been told he was sent to a family in the country. Connie's mother had told me the dog had been put to sleep.) I explained to her that the dog would not return, but I also encouraged her to write down her feelings as a way to help her with the loss. The next morning there was a letter on my desk. It gave an extremely articulate description of her feelings. When I spoke with Connie, she said the writing had made her feel better. I told her that writing about painful things can be helpful and urged her to keep a journal or to continue writing letters. I received several notes before school closed, but they were all happy and positive in tone.

I had a parent conference with Connie's father in April. He was late, and I had a conference scheduled right after with another parent so we weren't able to speak for very long. I thanked him for not continuing to pressure Connie about her multiplication tables and explained she had learned them by memory very quickly. His English was not as fluent as her mother's, so communication was somewhat difficult. I saw Connie's mother several times before the end of the semester picking up her children from childcare. She always said hello, but never seemed to have time to talk. She never again approached me regarding Connie's behavior or progress.

The semester is over; Connie is moving on to fourth grade and I have seen improvement and progress, but the situation continues to haunt me. I am constantly re-thinking my reactions to this child who in many ways would be considered an "ideal" student. Was the red flag alerting me to something? I think of the quote from Thoreau: "The mass of men lead lives of quiet desperation." Was this Connie? The question remains unanswered.

Lilly Siu, Teacher
San Francisco Unified School District

When I first read this teacher's case, I immediately thought of my own childhood because I could relate in many ways to the little girl Connie, who, like me, struggled between two worlds: the values and standards of her Chinese parents and her adopted San Franciscan life-style.

Like Connie, I have a younger brother, who I often felt got "better" treatment than myself. Like her, I resented it silently, all the while keeping respect for my parents by not bringing it up. Unlike Connie, however, I had sisters to talk to, sisters who could understand my resentment, but also explain why, if not because it was fair, it was simply going to be like this. In many Asian families, particularly Chinese, it is not uncommon for parents to favor sons. It comes from the patriarchal nature of the Chinese society itself. Sons carry on the family name, and in the interest of the family, that makes them more valuable.

Knowing the value of having someone to talk to, I think this teacher might have taken a more aggressive stance on pursuing counseling for Connie. Connie needs a place to talk, a place where she will NOT be judged, much less scolded, for her feelings. I suspect the place most like this is her own classroom, where Connie looks for someone who will be her number one best friend. Connie seems to be looking for someone who will like her second to none, in contrast to her competition with Martin at home. In all likelihood, it is because the teacher treats all her students fairly that Connie was able to pick up on the double standards regarding her brother. Also, it is probably because the teacher maintains a safe classroom environment that Connie felt this was the place to speak her mind.

Connie seems to be the ideal student, yet she will probably never feel as though she has her parents' complete approval, at least not compared to her brother.

For Connie, the answer seems to lie in her ability to work through her jealousy of her brother and her own self-assurance. Bringing things up to her parents seems to keep the problem muffled, while speaking to an objective third party might just help the problem go away. Her parents probably won't help Connie find counseling help, because Chinese families are very private about their family difficulties.

I truly hope Connie finds someone to talk to and soon — if not a professional counselor, then someone else with a friendly ear. Her parents have helped make her an academic success, but her success in life seems to rely on an acceptance of herself.

Sharon Nelson-Barber, Lecturer
Stanford University

This case raises important issues about conflicts between home and school life. How do the values imparted in Connie's home compare with those of her teacher or the school in general? What cultural norms may have determined how Connie resolves conflicts or shows respect for others? What traditions and attitudes underlie her interactive and interpretive styles? What happens when these differ from those her teacher anticipates? What are the criteria used to judge Connie's actions, as well as those of her parents? The teacher is correct in wanting to know more about Connie's psychological/emotional development; however, she must also know something about the cultural forces that may have influenced that development.

A growing number of studies support the notion that students of color respond most favorably to teachers who first develop strong personal relationships with them and, in so doing, act more "human" [c.f. Foster's (1987) study of black inner-city college students, Martz's (1981) and Scollon and Scollon's (1981) accounts of Native Alaskan students, and Low's and Scollon's (1982) descriptions of Chinese youth in San Francisco]. The Chinese teachers I interviewed recently agreed that the first month of school is well spent getting to know the parents. They say that how well they "know" each family can be a factor in their students' overall academic success because these relationships have a bearing on parental cooperativeness, parental perceptions of the school, and the amount of pressure parents place on students to do well. One Chinese educator further explained that spending time "getting to know" each family is especially useful when students have problems. Since many Chinese parents continue to hold traditional beliefs about education that include high academic expectations — if [Connie] didn't have her times tables memorized by the weekend, she would get spanked by her father — getting to know families first helps teachers communicate with parents more effectively. It can aid them in figuring out how to approach parents or even in choosing words that will not be offensive or penalize the children.

All too frequently, individuals from different backgrounds enter into conversations that just don't work, never really understanding what goes wrong. Many times this is because the problem goes beyond vocabulary to the manner in which the words are communicated. For example, Chinese parents are often offended by what they perceive as "forwardness" or "bluntness" on the part of Anglo teachers. Comments like "I think your child should learn to do X" or "your child is having a problem with X" are often construed by these parents as rude criticisms of their child-rearing practices. Anglo teachers who value assertiveness are confused by such responses and question why these parents "don't want to put the problem on the table" or "meet conflicts head-on." In such cases, established relationships create connections that say to the parents, "The teacher is on our side — she is not trying to change my child, but to help." For teachers it means learning to fashion suggestions in ways that are more compatible with parental expectations, e.g., "Maybe we need to do X" or "we'll try to make more time for working on . . ." or "you can help me work this out." Such suggestions, which are viewed as "positive," are far more effective than "negative" comments that imply to the parents they are "not good parents" or "haven't done their job."

Though Connie's teacher knew the value of making connections with parents and seemed to make every effort to do so, she may not have fully understood the competing expectations with which these parents and Connie seemed to struggle. Negative experiences with Anglo teachers in the past may explain why Connie's father met with the teacher "very briefly" and "appeared to be in a hurry and left quickly." Since the Chinese emphasize formality, and he didn't speak fluent English, he may have seen himself on uncomfortably unequal turf with the teacher. Unfortunately, how Anglo teachers sometimes interpret these "more reserved," "quiet," and "unemotional" behaviors are based on very different assumptions than those of many Chinese.

For example, in the teacher's estimation, Connie's mother displayed "emotional remoteness" toward her daughter when, in response to Connie's suicidal threats, she "gave her a hard lesson" and "spanked her." In addition, when the teacher observed Connie's emotional confrontation with her mother, the mother "seemed somewhat removed. . . retort[ing] each accusation calmly. . .mixing Chinese and English." The difference is that from a Western point of view, such actions suggest great insensitivity and even meanness. From a Chinese point of view, they suggest care and concern for the appropriate upbringing of the child.

According to the California State Department of Education's *Handbook for Teaching Cantonese-Speaking Students* (1984), many Chinese parents believe that discipline is central to a well-rounded education and that the school should play an important role in reinforcing the values and codes of conduct taught in the home. Along with values that emphasize reserve and formality come a demand for restraint, inhibition of strong feelings, and above all, obedience to authority. If Connie was raised in a home in which she is expected to restrain her feelings and in which misbehavior in public is unacceptable and an embarrassment to her parents, crossing her mother in front of her teacher represented a complete breach of manners. The mother was obliged to show little emotion and "calmly" soothe the child into more appropriate behavior. Connie was also obliged to "apologize" for "making [the teacher] feel bad."

Caught between two worlds, as it seems she is, Connie must be confused about the competing messages fostered at school and at home. Her teacher and principal, who appear to value spontaneity and informality, try to come up with various ways to help Connie vent her frustrations. Since her teacher frequently invited Connie to talk about her problems, she may have asked why not share her anger about Sparky and complain about her brother being able to "do what he wants"? Of course, her parents didn't seem to see it this way. Her principal voluntarily met with Connie, intending to provide a comfortable place for her to voice her feelings. However, given the highly prescribed notions of authority in her home culture, it is not surprising Connie believed she was "in serious trouble because she had been sent to the principal." All of these competing forces may explain why Connie's parents "never again approached [the teacher] regarding Connie's behavior or progress."

Even though the teacher faced many obstacles throughout the year, it seems she was beginning to make progress with Connie. She was able to assure the parents that Connie was a good student, which alleviated some of the unneeded pressure placed on her at home. She also urged Connie to begin writing about her feelings in a journal, which clearly "made her feel better," yet did not conflict with her parents' notions of public and private face. It is just unfortunate that this caring teacher had to spend so much time learning how to make the right connections.

Learning to communicate across differences represents one of the most important tasks that teachers face in today's multiethnic classrooms. Such diversity means that teachers must have a willingness to reflect on their own ways of knowing and doing, to be able to ask questions, and to know where to begin to look for some of the answers.

[The author wishes to acknowledge the thoughtful counsel of Irene Dea Collier and Calvin Toy.]

REFERENCES

California State Department of Education, Bilingual Education Office. (1984). *A handbook for teaching Cantonese-speaking students*. Sacramento, CA: California State Department of Education.

Foster, M. (1987). *It's cookin' now: A performance analysis of the speech events of a black teacher in an urban community college* (Doctoral thesis). Cambridge, MA: Harvard University, Graduate School of Education.

Low, V. (1982). *The unimpressible race: A century of educational struggle by the Chinese in San Francisco.* San Francisco: East/West Publishing Co.

Martz, C. (1981). *You are welcome: A study of cross-cultural sensitivity in four university classrooms* (Master's thesis). Fairbanks, AK: University of Alaska, Center for Cross-Cultural Studies.

Scollon, R., & Scollon, S. (1981). *Narrative literacy and face in interethnic communication.* Norwood, NJ: Ablex.

Alice A. Kawazoe, Staff Development & Curriculum Director Oakland Unified School District

This case presents such a tangle of emotions, repression, expression, cultural conflicts, and personal needs. What complicates the issues is that we recognize some aspects of ourselves reflected in Connie — the need to be a *best* friend, not just one of a group, the desire to feel special and singular in someone's eyes, and the resentment when another is favored; but Connie seems to push each reaction to disturbing extremes.

Many of us, as children and maybe as adults, too, have threatened to run away, disappear, or do ourselves in. When I was eight, I made a half-hearted, but dramatic attempt at suicide by jumping off the porch yelling, "You'll be sorry when I'm dead," interested more in my family's reaction to my demise than the act itself. But few of us at five years old have threatened to cut our wrists because a friend would not play with us anymore. A psychiatrist or a psychologist might say that this type of threat is a symptom rather than a cause of an illness. A mental health professional, sensitive to the cultural and psychological context of Asian families, needs to counsel Connie and her family to discern the causes of her behavior and to help her resolve her conflicts.

Another aspect of this case that interests, though not surprises me is the tension between private upset and public exposure of that upset. The trip to the principal's office was probably a shameful experience for Connie and Mai Ling and an alarming one for their parents; being sent to the principal denotes "serious trouble."

Connie's outburst in front of her teacher and her mother may have been disconcerting for the teacher, but was probably appalling for the mother. Connie spills out her anger and resentment about the giving away of her dog without being told, not being permitted to put pictures on the walls or talk on the telephone, the preferential treatment her brother receives, and the stealing of her letters. All this backlog of resentment boils up and out.

Now she doesn't have a best friend; she is in trouble at school; her teacher is upset; her mother is frustrated; she does not feel loved. Connie has become an emotional volcano.

What the teacher interprets as a "calm" or "removed" reaction in the mother, might well be embarrassment or shame, shame the mother feels about her daughter's explosion and the waving in public of her private anguish. Understandably, in those tense moments, she relies on the privacy of Chinese to talk to her daughter. The mother thought she had resolved the suicide issue when Connie was five by giving her the "hard lesson" of a spanking, and she might see Connie's present anger as another "in-house" issue, to be dealt with at home within the family, and not a school problem to be worked out with the teacher or principal.

Given these familial sensibilities, it is not surprising then that after discussion of the situation at home, Connie apologizes for making the teacher "feel bad." She is apologizing on behalf of herself and her parents for subjecting the teacher to an uncomfortable experience and for forcing the teacher to witness her personal feelings.

I don't have any quick response or facile suggestions about this case. This is one of those larger-than-school, too-serious-for-one-teacher-to-handle-alone situations. These experiences will continue to haunt us because we cannot ever sever the threads that bind school life to home life and personal life. The interweaving of these strands creates a textured fabric, but often, too, the threads tangle, forming knots not easily loosened.

Case 13

Home Visits

It was spring, and the big Saturday had finally come. All year the intermediate grades children in my inner-city San Francisco school's arts program had rehearsed for a production at the city's well-known outdoor performance stage, set in a scenic eucalyptus grove. Excitement ran high. Earlier, we teachers had voiced a word of caution: it may be wise, we said, to send a bus to transport children who lived in the housing projects. But the organizers of the event — volunteers from a nonprofit arts agency — felt sure that parents wouldn't let their children miss so important an opportunity.

The morning fog gave way to sunshine. Stage decorations went up as scheduled. The audience had already begun to assemble. But at the hour when all the children had been told to be there, over 15 — all from the projects — hadn't shown up. The frantic organizers called me to see if there was anything I could do to avert a crisis.

I have taught intermediate grades for 25 years in inner-city, multi-racial settings. My own background is mixed minority,[8] and I was raised in a multi-racial setting in downtown Los Angeles. Both my personal and professional experience bolster my firm belief that all parents care about their children, even if they never set foot in the school. At this school, as in many other urban settings, we have busing, and what that mainly means is that parents are not accessible the way they used to be. You sometimes have to go to them. As I drove toward the projects, I felt grateful that I had laid some careful groundwork, and I hoped that my outreach efforts would work to the children's advantage this day.

I have a policy of calling every family during the first two weeks of school. (This is workable, since there usually aren't more than 30 students in my class.) I introduce myself; talk a little about the curriculum, field trips, conflict resolution program, and camping trips;

_____

[8] The case author's ethnic background is Native American and white, and she was raised in a Latino community.

and I invite parents to join us whenever they feel like it. I always ask if there's anything special they think I should know about their child, since we're going to be so close this year.

If I can't get hold of a child's parents by phone or note, I go to them. Sometimes phones are disconnected, and sometimes parents have had bad experiences with school and shy away from contact. I feel it's important to bridge that gap; we're working together for the good of one young person.

The key is to make the circumstances of the visit pleasant, so that the experience is a good one for me, the student, and the parents. Because of busing, my visit may entail a ride across town to an unfamiliar neighborhood. If it's a high crime neighborhood, common sense dictates against going at night. I may instead have someone meet me there on a Saturday morning. But I go.

I never walk up to a home unannounced; that's rude, and makes the school look like the police. I send a note home and ask for an appointment. If I don't get an answer, I check the address and see if the family lives near anyone I know. If they do, I call and ask that person to talk to the parent, maybe even arrange for the visit to take place at the neighbor's home. Some people don't want the school in their house because they're afraid or embarrassed; I don't feel it's my business to pry into their private situation. I just want to talk to them about their child.

If I still can't get the parent, I go to the "Power Mom." Every neighborhood has the lady who knows everything about everybody. She can be your most trusted and valuable ally. Far from a busybody, she is a cherished person, usually called "Grandma" by young and old alike. Ask any child who the nicest neighbor lady is, and if they live near each other, they all say the same name. These wonderful women have clued me in on children's backgrounds and behaviors, and have helped me with

classroom management and in my own personal understanding of children's problems and needs. The Power
Mom is likely to know all about the people I want to
contact; often, she can have them ready to meet with me
within hours.

Each neighborhood also has some after-school gym,
recreational, or tutorial program. In an hour I can drive
over, look around, meet the directors or tutors, and see
the children in action. The children love it that I visit
them on their own turf, the rec or tutorial leaders love it
that the school is interested, and the parents definitely
hear about it. For very little time, it's good public
relations.

These things can be done by any teacher, regardless of
race or color. The one other teacher in my school doing
similar home outreach is white. The payoffs, we find, are
enormous. For personal safety, a major benefit is being
recognized in the neighborhood. About three years ago,
for example, after a late field trip, I was dropping off a
parent and seven children in a predominantly black
housing project with a fairly dangerous reputation. As I
went to drive away, a line of about 12 youths sprang up
in front of my car. I stopped. One yelled something and
pointed to my left front tire. I rolled down the window,
and he said, "This tire looks flat. Better get out and check
it." A classic robbery setup. I was debating backing up
fast or trying to run through their line when one of the
older youths came closer, stared, and said, "The teacher!"
They stepped away, like the parting of the Red Sea.

As for classroom benefits, if the family knows you, even
superficially, problems don't arise as much with the
children. There is nothing more empowering than
saying to a disruptive child, "You know, your mother
and I were talking the other day. . ." This sentence has
caused more children than I can number to re-evaluate
their behavior in an instant. When a problem does come
up, a home visit can bring surprises all around. Once, I
thought a child was stealing. I called her home. Her
grandmother asked if I could come to the house and tell

the mother in person. I drove over on a Saturday morning and found that my student lived with three generations of women in a small but cheerful and comfortable
space. When I met the girl's great grandmother, my plan
instantly changed. She was so dignified and obviously
religious that I felt it would humiliate her if I accused
her great granddaughter of theft. Instead, to the obvious
relief of my student, we discussed the elderly woman's
childhood, her dreams for her girls, and some assignments my student could do at home to bring up her
grades. We located a quiet homework location. The next
day, all the missing items were on my desk, and I had a
friend for life.

All of this was on my mind that Saturday as I approached the projects with little time to spare. For the
sake of efficiency, I went right to Grandma Bessie. When
she saw me coming up the walkway, she called merrily
out the window, "So they sent the big gun, did they?" I
had to laugh. She was pleased and flattered that I came
to her. She also knew without asking why I was there.
Within 15 minutes, we had all the kids but one (whose
mother simply wouldn't get up). I had teachers with
other cars on the way, and the long-awaited performance was saved.

*Case 13
Commentaries*

*Joan Tibbetts, Teacher
San Francisco Unified School District*

During this past year, while I was acting as a resource teacher, I have had many occasions to visit this teacher. Each time I entered her room, I was struck by the students' heightened sense of interest and involvement. I also noticed the mutual respect the students and teacher seemed to have for each other. Not only did this teacher interact with the families, but she, with her students, extended this involvement further by going out into the community to help those in need.

In my years as an educator, I have always felt that each child needs very personal attention. It's long been very clear that students' problems in concentrating and learning often stem from troubles at home. I remember a six-year-old girl in special education who came clear across her school after the dismissal bell to tell me she was afraid her mother was going to be killed. She opened up and told me a number of frightening things that were happening in her home. Another child, a fifth grade boy, had been suspended several times for going into different classrooms at recess and stealing food. One day he came to me in tears. He told me that there was practically never any food at home and most of the time he was very hungry. Then there were the five or six kindergarten children who huddled under my coat one very cold, windy day. They told me how cold they were; they didn't own any coats or jackets.

I tried to help these children and the many others who asked for help in reading and learning. But their concerns exceeded what the school context could offer. For those with the most severe problems, I kept asking myself, "How can they learn? How can they concentrate?" I wanted to see if I could help in some way, so I contacted the families. At first, I asked if I could come to their homes and tutor.

I am white. There were those from the Establishment who warned me that home visits might be dangerous and that I wouldn't be accepted. But I wasn't afraid. I felt that since each student I worked with was unique and special, their families must be too. On my first few visits, however, I did experience some anger and hostility in the neighborhoods. But as the families started taking me into their confidence, so too did the relatives, then the neighbors. People began treating me with great warmth and graciousness. One visit especially touched me deeply. A fourth grade boy had assembled all his relatives — aunts and uncles and cousins — to greet me when I arrived.

One day, while I was showing some young children how to prepare their backyard plot to plant vegetables, two boys of about 16 or 17 wandered up. They stood there shifting from one foot to the other. They said they'd been suspended from school. "Would you like to help us?" I asked. In a flash they jumped over the fence, "took to" the hoes and shovels, and had a great time. Before they left, they asked if I would mind helping them and their families set up gardens.

Still, I continued to be upset by the families who live in a perpetual state of hunger, cold, emotional deprivation, or terror. One day after school, I arrived at a home just as four young hungry teens burst in calling, "I'm hungry!" The mother opened the refrigerator; the only thing in it was one piece of bread. As she cut it into four pieces, I saw her look of hopelessness. She said to me, "What am I to do?"

I started helping as many people as I could by getting needed food, collecting clothes, and helping individuals look for work. Most important, I encouraged people and told them they had a great deal to offer. Repeatedly, I've seen that people — adults and children — who get an extra "pat on the back" and are made to feel that their lives really do count for something, respond by starting to believe in themselves. Grades go up; students can take more interest in school; adults have the courage to go out and look for work.

My experience shows me that schools can gain much by reaching out to families and showing them that they are critically important in their child's education. During this past school year alone, I was overwhelmed when over 200 students asked for my help with reading, other studies, or problems. I couldn't possibly help them all. Out of that frustration grew my summer "help each other" program, strongly dependent on family participation.

I targeted the program on students having the greatest difficulty with reading. Many of these kids were tagged non-readers. I called the families and asked if they would be interested in being involved. Most were wary. They seemed to be thinking, "Is this for real? My child really can't learn to read."

After several weeks of my working with the students at school and the families working with them at home, the families started expressing surprise and gratitude that these children were reading, showing signs of dramatic progress, and gaining confidence.

I think of one mother in particular. When I first contacted her, she reacted with anger and suspicion. She thought I was just another person calling to say something negative about her son. Her son had been called a troublemaker, a slow learner, a non-reader. When I told her I believed in him and his ability to learn, she agreed to participate. One day, several weeks into the program, as I drove up to her house, she came rushing out, all smiles, saying, "He can read! My son can read!" She went on to tell me that he was gaining so much confidence that the whole family would gather in the evenings and he would read out loud to them.

Like the teacher in this case, I'd seen what's possible when families see that someone really does care.

Sharon Nelson-Barber, Lecturer
Stanford University

This case beautifully illustrates the importance of teachers' having an enlarged role in the lives of their students. As the racial, ethnic, and socioeconomic diversity of our nation's classrooms continues to broaden, so also do the day-to-day challenges of teaching. In many urban centers, the complex matrix of multilingual/multicultural students, changing societal values, and the deficiencies of the schools themselves, place heavy burdens on traditional education's efforts to address the unique needs of these students and their settings. Teaching in today's classrooms often means going beyond "the content to be taught" to the relationship of that content to students' broader contexts — their social environments, their attitudes, even their feelings. Many teachers claim that some of the elements most critical to their success in these settings are the ability to draw upon local values and expectations about teaching and learning and the ability to forge meaningful relationships with their students — skills not necessarily honed within the confines of the school.

It was the fruits of just such "careful groundwork" that the teacher in this case counted on that Saturday morning as she "approached the projects with little time to spare." Her valiant efforts to establish trust with her students' families through personal contacts and by maintaining a high degree of visibility in the community paid off in a variety of ways. For families accustomed to outsiders' intolerance and fear of their communities, her willingness to venture into "unfamiliar neighborhoods" affirmed her commitment to the schooling of their children. Her determination to meet with families helped her to earn credibility as a "real" and "caring" person who did not confuse her students' circumstances of poverty, their race, or ethnicity with potential to achieve in school.

These activities not only contributed to her ability to enlist the help of key community figures like the neighborhood Power Mom; it also accorded her a high level of respect, as evidenced when the 12 questionable youths recognized her as "the teacher" and "stepped away like the parting of the Red Sea." In the classroom she found that she often could maintain discipline by uttering something as simple as "Your mother and I were talking the other day...," which allowed more time to get on with the business of teaching. On the morning of the school arts program production, when over 15 student participants hadn't shown up, she was able to call upon her carefully crafted affiliation with families to "save" the event.

Such direct personal involvement is very meaningful to families who feel ignored or believe that they have little voice in the educational decisions made for their children. For even though most teachers are well-intentioned, their lack of awareness about community and cultural styles and norms often prevents the kind of meaningful communication parents require to become full participants in their children's school lives. If by the parents' standards teachers appear distanced and insensitive, they may well fail to cooperate and "not want the school in their house."

Unfortunately, such actions spark a vibrant chorus of misconceptions about poor and minority parents' responses to traditional schooling. A recurring theme is the notion that these parents don't "care" about their children's education. Teacher attestations range from comments that the students' parents don't come to back-to-school night or attend parent-teacher conferences, to the notion that these students come from undisciplined homes, to observations that many parents send their children to school when they are sick, but do not seem to care about their attendance when they are well.

What many teachers do not stop to think about (or in many cases have not been prepared to think about) are alternative explanations for these and other scenarios that arise in diverse classrooms. As this teacher writes, "even if [parents] never set foot in school," the teacher should not make judgments until she is sure those judgments are based on the correct underlying assumptions.

One assumption that mainstream educators seem to take for granted is that the same education should be offered to all children. Lately, of course, it has become increasingly clear that all children do not come to school equally prepared to learn within the frame provided by the school. According to Delpit (1988), parents from many non-mainstream communities ask that the schools offer their children the mainstream "cultural" content they cannot provide at home. For example, she says that poor black parents want their children to acquire the discourse patterns, interactional styles, and spoken and written language codes that will allow them more opportunities for success in the larger society. However, teachers must take this knowledge one step farther and ask whether parents unfamiliar with these styles and patterns may feel underprepared or even intimidated by contexts like back-to-school night or one-to-one conferences, where they may believe they are on uncomfortably unequal turf with the teacher.

In Native-American communities the issues become even more thorny when traditional models of instruction require teachers to organize, conduct, and reward students in ways that conflict with indigenous community values. The consequence here is that native students are frequently penalized for behaviors that reflect appropriate socialization into their own culture. For example, should conflicts arise in school (a misunderstanding with the teacher or another student), children accustomed to removing themselves from uncomfortable situations believe it is perfectly acceptable to leave the school entirely as a way to resolve the problem. Children raised to be careful observers and trusted to make their own decisions about personal needs are often confused by elaborate management systems strictly bounded by clocks, bells, and teacher directives, and may pay little attention to teachers who command them to "get a drink now" or "be sure to return to your seat in one minute." Locust (1988) explains that native families who live in harsh environments can be accustomed to living with minor physical discomforts and therefore may be less concerned about sending their children to school with a runny nose or a cough. She points out that the more serious problem in the eyes of these native parents would be the school's failure to recognize "spiritual unwellness" (which may or may not have visible symptoms) as an excusable illness.

Most certainly, teachers cannot know all things about all students from all backgrounds. It seems a far better idea to prepare teachers to develop a range of responses to "new" behaviors that subsume the understanding that "problems" often have more to do with the school's own cultural presuppositions than with individual students or their families. Spending time in the community and learning about students' home and community lives can help teachers reexamine their own assumptions as well as the ways in which they make judgments about their students' abilities. Being visible and showing they care about their students can help to establish the personal connections that are more likely to engage parents and elicit their help. As the present case shows, "home visits" represent one step in the right direction for acquiring such knowledge.

REFERENCES

Delpit, L. (1988). The silenced dialogue: Power and pedagogy in educating other peoples' children. *Harvard Educational Review, 58*(3), 280-298.

Locust, C. (1988). Wounding the spirit: Discrimination and traditional American Indian belief systems. *Harvard Educational Review, 58*(3), 315-330.

ANNOTATED BIBLIOGRAPHY

Cohen, Elizabeth G. (1986). *Designing groupwork: Strategies for the heterogeneous classroom.* New York: Teacher's College Press.

In this book on cooperative learning, Cohen advocates her version of "groupwork" — an instructional method that allows students in heterogeneous classrooms to learn primarily from each other regardless of differing levels of achievement, cultural distinctions, or race. Unlike other works on the same subject, *Designing Groupwork* provides specific "interventions" that equalize interaction between students of differing status. Blending theory and practice, it introduces general concepts, presents research documenting the useful effects of groupwork practices, and then provides classroom activities that capitalize on the power of this new method.

Delpit, Lisa D. (1986). Skills and other dilemmas of a progressive black educator. *Harvard Educational Review, 56*(4), 379-385.

Delpit candidly describes her own "progressive" education, her professional practice, and how she gradually came to believe that many aspects of "good" teaching deny black students a full education. She also describes minority teachers' feelings of estrangement from the progressive process approach to teaching writing, urging its leaders to develop a vocabulary that includes educators with differing perspectives. Delpit shares her view that writing teachers need to fuse process and skills approaches for success with black students. A subsequent article, *The Silenced Dialogue,* expands on and adds to these views.

Delpit, Lisa D. (1988). The silenced dialogue: Power and pedagogy in educating other people's children. *Harvard Educational Review, 58*(3), 280-298.

In this article, Delpit addresses the "culture of power" — codes or rules used to gain power in society — and white educators' failure to teach these implicit social codes to black students. Referring to her 1986 article *Skills and Other Dilemmas,* she argues that "progressive" white educators often fail to transmit the spoken and written language codes of mainstream culture in an effort to avoid disempowering their students. The result, she says, is the opposite. She concludes that educators must be direct and explicit with black students in order to meet their educational needs, but must also validate and allow students to explore their own "expertness."

Guthrie, Grace Pung. (1985). *A school divided: An ethnography of bilingual education in a Chinese community.* Hillsdale, NJ: Lawrence Erlbaum Associates.

Guthrie addresses issues of ethnolinguistic identity, pluralism, and assimilation in this multi-level ethnography of a 10-year-old English/Chinese bilingual program in the heart of "Little Canton," a Chinese-American community in California. Through a series of first-hand observations and interviews, Guthrie portrays the initiation, implementation, and eventual perceptions of the bilingual program at the classroom, program, school, and community levels. She points out the dangers of indiscriminately transferring models of bilingual education from one ethnic group to another, and identifies the complexities of eliciting agreement from parents about the goals of such bilingual programs. *A School Divided* shows how the dynamics of a community, its history and its aspirations play a significant role in issues as fundamental as whether a bilingual educational program is even necessary. Foreword by J.U. Ogbu.

Heath, Shirley Brice. (1983). *Ways with words: Language, life, and work in communities and classrooms*. New York: Cambridge University Press.

Heath relates insights gleaned from 10 years' observation of the lives and language development patterns of children from two working-class communities — one black, one white — in the Southeastern United States. Through intimate contact with members of each of these communities, she studied the ways their children acquire language at home. Her book describes the deep cultural differences that result. Further differences between the two communities and the townspeople ("mainstreamers") give both groups difficulty in schools controlled by mainstream educators, both black and white. *Ways with Words* urges educators to better understand their students' ingrained language habits and to use ethnography to break the communication barrier between communities and classrooms.

King, Joyce Elaine, & Ladson-Billings, Gloria. (1990). The teacher education challenge in elite university settings: Developing critical perspectives for teaching in a democratic and multicultural society. *European Journal of Intercultural Studies*, 1(2), 15-30.

The authors describe in explicit detail their theory of emancipatory education and their work instructing education students to develop socially critical perspectives and multicultural competencies consistent with democratic values, social justice and emancipatory, or socially equitable, education. In a process of self-discovery, self-assessment, knowledge and action, graduate and undergraduate students explore their conceptions of race and education as they affect both teacher and student in the classroom. The authors present citations and theories, then trace specific activities carried out in an effort to better prepare teacher candidates for socially transformational work in urban, diverse settings.

Ladson-Billings, Gloria, & Henry, Annette. (1990, Fall). Blurring the borders: Voices of African liberatory pedagogy in the United States and Canada. *Journal of Education*, 172(2) 72-88.

Using data from two studies — one conducted in the United States and one in Canada — the authors conclude that successful teachers of black students are engaged in "culturally relevant pedagogy." Teachers using this pedagogy infuse both their own and their students' cultural knowledge to ensure academic, social, and cultural success. Ethnographic interviews and classroom observations capture the voices of black teachers, who, with their multiple consciousness of race, gender, class, and nationality, offer insights for teacher educators and teachers of black students.

Michaels, Sarah. (1986). Narrative presentations: An oral preparation for literacy with first graders. In *The Social Construction of Literacy*, pp. 94-116. Cambridge: Cambridge University Press.

Through a linguistic study of narrative styles, Michaels systematically demonstrates stable though seemingly unconscious patterns of differential treatment of black children. Describing a highly collaborative classroom activity between student and teacher — sharing time — she points out communicative mismatches such as differing narrative schemata, lack of a shared sense of topic, and apparent misreading of prosodic clues by a white classroom teacher. The result is unsuccessful collaboration and misassessment of black children's ability. Michaels suggests that a first step toward improved collaboration is awareness that these children's styles are logical and regular.

Nelson-Barber, Sharon. (1990). Considerations for the inclusion of multiple cultural competencies in teacher assessment: A Yup'ik Eskimo case. *Canadian Journal of Native Education, 17*(2), 33-42.

Working from the premise that cultural biases on standardized tests exclude a large number of minority candidates from the teaching profession, Nelson-Barber asserts that teacher education and assessment must tap and promote cultural understandings to fairly and equally assess all teachers. Through collaborative work between the Teacher Assessment Project (TAP) at Stanford University and a group of native Yup'ik teachers from Alaska, Nelson-Barber reports the teachers' conclusion that the National Board for Professional Standards should embellish its standards with culturally appropriate information and procedures and hold teachers accountable for multiple cultural competencies. The teachers then describe helpful competencies and activities necessary for work in Yup'ik or any diverse classroom, giving the reader and the Board concrete suggestions for improving assessment of *all* teachers.

Nelson-Barber, Sharon, & Meier, Terry. (1990, Spring). Multicultural context a key factor in teaching. *Academic Connections*, pp. 1-5, 9-11.

Citing numerous studies and specific examples, the authors provide a very readable introduction to successful practice with multicultural students and the problems caused by cultural incongruence between educators and their students. They illustrate two main points: 1) how achievement by poor or minority students often results from their middle-class, white teacher's failure to understand and incorporate students' cultural-specific styles of interaction and learning in the classroom, and 2) this failure often leads teachers and administrators to inappropriately judge poor or minority students to have behavioral problems, academic deficiencies, or learning disabilities.

Nembhard, Judith P. (1983). A perspective on teaching black dialect speaking students to write standard English. *Journal of Negro Education, 52*(1), 75-82.

Nembhard describes and reviews the broad spectrum of conflicting opinions about the need for and methods of teaching "black dialect speakers" to write in standard English. She covers the misdirected goal of eradication, bidialectism as advocated by some linguists, an apparently successful writing process approach, prejudice manifested in methods, and some teaching failures. She then presents a list of her own recommendations for writing programs serving black students, stressing that teachers must show confidence in and have high expectations for students. Despite theories to the contrary, she concludes that requiring black students to become proficient in standard English is not a denial of their background and heritage.

Olsen, Laurie. (1988). *Crossing the schoolhouse border: Immigrant students and the California public schools.* San Francisco: California Tomorrow.

This landmark report documents the varied and often painful experiences of immigrant children in California, the nature of programs designed to serve them, and California's unique opportunity to create a richly diverse and educated state. Through 360 interviews in 33 California communities with immigrant children and educators, the report explores in detail the experiences of children struggling to swim and not sink in the school system. Some escape war; most undergo culture shock. Yet, many excel through hard work and determination. Programs serving these students are shown to be woefully inadequate, and their staffs are often overwhelmed. The report concludes with a long list of recommendations from an array of sources, ranging from the governor to community advocacy organizations.

Simonson, Rick, & Walker, Scott. (1988). *The Graywolf annual five: Multicultural literacy.* St. Paul: Graywolf Press.

This collection of 13 short essays responds to several contemporary works which cite the deficiencies of the American school system and call for a "back-to-basics" curriculum. The authors argue that "cultural literacy" (or "what every American should know") cannot ignore the contributions of women and people of color in the United States. They also argue that any revised curriculum should embrace both traditional Western classics and the classics of non-European cultures such as those of Africa, Asia, and Latin America. Authors include James Baldwin, Carlos Fuentes, Michelle Cliff, and Ishmael Reed. The book suggests a "beginning list" of names, places, dates, and concepts that a literate individual should know in our multicultural society.

Smitherman, Geneva. (n.d.). Talkin' and testifyin' about black dialect: Past, present, and future tense. *Teaching English, Journal of the National Council of Teachers of English*, 66-74.

Smitherman describes three schools of thought concerning the teaching of standard English to black dialect speakers — all the while switching in and out of standard, academic language, and "the dialect of her nurture." She dismisses the eradicationist and bidialectalist approaches, contending that they inappropriately differentiate the two styles of speaking, and thereby perpetuate linguistic and social oppression. She claims that a teacher of English "legitimizes" by teaching kids to compose rhetorically powerful oral and/or written communication in their own linguistically and socially valid form. She presents ideas concerning attitude and methods of imparting communication skills and, more specifically, speaking skills such as media or audio/oral/visual processes instruction, but concludes that writing instruction should not be stressed except as a tool to organize thought.

Trueba, Henry T., Guthrie, Grace Pung, & Au, Kathryn Hu-Pei (Eds.). (1981). *Culture and the bilingual classroom: Studies in classroom ethnography.* Rowley, MA: Newbury House.

This collection of papers is a survey of current issues in ethnography and bilingual education. Their introduction argues for cultural pluralism — coexistence of different cultures on an equal basis — in the classroom and the larger society in place of America's current structural pluralism or differential distribution of rights between groups. Theoretical and methodological works include Erickson's *Approaches to Inquiry* and Hymes' *Ethnographic Monitoring* — which further elaborates the importance of ethnographic research in bilingual education. Studies include Mohatt and Erickson's examination of significant cultural differences in interaction patterns of Odawa Indian classrooms, and Van Ness's analysis of social organization in getting ready for reading in an Athabaskan classroom. These studies show culture to be a critical variable in cross-cultural classrooms; most

significantly, Mohatt and Erickson find that
systematic cultural differences survive even with
children whose first and only language is
English. This collection is useful primarily for
researchers and teacher educators, but can also
be helpful to teachers interested in exploring
how knowledge of implicit cultural codes can
lead to greater cultural understanding.

Trueba, Henry T., Jacobs, Lila, & Kirton, Elizabeth.
(1990). *Cultural conflict and adaptation: The case of
Hmong children in American society.* Bristol, PA: The
Falmer Press.

The authors address cultural conflict in America
and American schools through the historical and
day-to-day struggles of a group of Indochinese
Hmong refugees and the small California
elementary school responsible for educating the
Hmong children. Using ethnographic field-
based research, this book is intended to provide
educators frustrated by a lack of cultural understanding with some insights into the nature of
cultural conflict in ethnically diverse schools.
The authors focus on problems of educational
equity, instructional effectiveness, and cultural
sensitivity to the diverse ethnic groups represented in public schools. They also provide
theoretical and historical background on the
Hmong, and explore issues of minority cultures
and achievement in American schools and
society.

Guidelines for Writing a Case

The casebook provides a way of capturing two kinds of teacher knowledge. One is the knowledge about learning the basics of classroom teaching. The second is the cultural knowledge that teachers have gained by working in diverse settings. Both kinds of knowledge can be passed on to beginning and experienced teachers who teach students in our increasingly multicultural environment.

Cases are used in many professions, both to prepare novices for their new role and to make available and accessible a body of knowledge. Unlike law and medicine, teaching traditionally has not had a case literature. Educators have not had a mechanism to accumulate the wealth of knowledge that teachers possess. As a result, we leave no legacy for those who follow us.

The Far West Laboratory's Institute for Case Development addresses this situation. Its work supports teachers who wish to contribute to the literature on teaching, currently dominated by researchers. Our first product, *The Mentor Teacher Casebook*, includes cases written by mentor teachers in the Los Angeles Unified School District (LAUSD) about their work with beginning teachers. That book accumulated a set of cases that can be passed on as a legacy to new mentors. The next casebook, *The Intern Teacher Casebook*, incorporates narratives written by beginning teachers in LAUSD that describe situations and problems that confront all novices during their early months of teaching. Both of these volumes are being used by LAUSD, other school districts, universities, and state departments of education around the country as tools for professional development with both new and experienced teachers.

This current volume, *Diversity in the Classroom*, is aimed at helping teachers who are unprepared to deal effec-

tively with either poverty or the linguistic and ethnic diversity in their classes. We hope that these narratives with their accompanying layers of commentary provide teacher educators and staff developers with the tools they need to promote discussion about alternative ways to effectively teach diverse youngsters.

WHAT DO WE MEAN BY A CASE?

A case is not merely a narrative or description of any particular event or series of events. Rather, we make a theoretical claim that it is a "case of something." Persons interested in writing cases may select from 16 the sample topics here, such as "teaching a new idea" or "teacher-student conflict" (see below). Each case tells a story. It describes what led up to the teaching event and the consequences that follow the event. To the extent possible, it also describes how the participants in the event were thinking and feeling.

WRITING A CASE

A compelling case should be built around a problem, a challenge, or a dilemma that may be common to many teachers. It's best to select a problem where your first attempt to deal with the problem didn't work. You tried to resolve it with several alternatives before succeeding or giving up. Try to think of a situation where questions can be raised about how best to approach a problem.

TOPICS FOR YOUR CASE.

Beginnings: One of the recurring challenges for both new and veteran teachers is figuring out how to begin things.

1) **Starting the school year.** How do you begin a school year with a new group of students? Tell the story of how you began a particular year with a particular group of kids. Describe the students and the ways that you attempted to bring the contributions of

their home and community to your classroom. Were there any surprises? Be sure to include any modifications you may have made to accommodate unexpected student responses.

2) **Starting the school day.** How do you begin a school day (or period)? How, if at all, do your routines reflect the ethnic backgrounds of your students? Tell your story, focusing on a particular day or period. Were there any surprises? Be sure to include any modifications you have made to unexpected student responses.

3) **Teaching a new idea.** Think about a specific lesson or unit during which you wanted to teach something new. Describe what you intended to teach. Did you attempt to do anything to use the students' contributions from their home and/or community in your plans? Tell your story. How did the students respond? Did you modify any planned strategies to respond to your students? Do you have any lingering questions about your lesson/unit?

4) **Receiving a new student.** A new student arrived in your classroom. How do you typically handle this situation? What happened in this case? Tell your story.

5) **Teaching a new class.** You were assigned to a school or class which includes students or backgrounds with which you are unfamiliar. You felt uncomfortable because of the differences. Tell your story. How did you deal with the situation?

Midcourse Challenges or Crises: These are the challenges that all new and veteran teachers face during a year.

6) **Teaching difficult content.** You prepared a lesson during which you wanted to explain a difficult concept or skill, but the kids didn't understand it. Describe the event. Did you do anything to attempt

to use the contributions of your students' home and/or community in your lesson? How did the kids respond? What did you do? Do you have any lingering questions?

7) **Interactions with difficult students.** You had a class where an individual or group of students refused to do work and were reluctant to participate in classroom activities. They either persistently acted out and caused trouble or were withdrawn and apathetic towards school. As a result, they weren't successful academically. You tried several different approaches to change their behavior, including possibly changing your expectations in some way, but the kids continued to cause problems. Or, your new strategies paid off. Tell your story.

8) **Teacher-student conflict.** You were involved in a conflict with a student or group of students. Describe the conflict. What do you think contributed to the situation? How did you handle it? Was there any resolution? How often do conflicts like this happen?

9) **Student-student conflict.** You had students in your class who have had a conflict with other students because of their diversity. Tell your story, using the above questions as prompts.

10) **Students with limited English.** You had students whose English is limited or who do not speak standard English. Tell your story, focusing on a particular student or group of students. How did the student(s) respond to your strategies?

11) **Students with minimal home support.** You had a student or group of students who come from families who were unable to provide nurturing and academic support. How do you deal with this situation? Be sure to include any modifications you may have made to accommodate these circumstances.

12) **Challenges of diversity**. As you taught a lesson or unit, you came to understand the meaning of the behavior of some of your students who are culturally or linguistically different. Describe your lesson or unit, your interactions with your students, and your insights into the behavior of your students. Do you still have any lingering questions?

Collaborations: What kinds of collaborative activities do you promote in your classroom and/or school?

13) **Student collaboration**. You tried a cooperative activity (e.g., small group, pairs) that was either very successful or quite unsuccessful. Describe the content and purpose of the lesson. Why did you select this kind of activity to teach? Describe how you planned for the activity, making sure that you include how you decided on the composition of each group. What happened? Do you have any lingering questions about this lesson?

14) **Teacher collaboration**. You collaborated with another teacher or group of teachers (e.g., to teach a lesson or unit that incorporates diversity, to plan a special activity that uses the contributions of your students' diverse backgrounds, to engage in mutual observation with another teacher). Tell your story. What were the consequences of the collaborative activity?

15) **Collaboration with community**. You collaborated with parents or local citizens/businesses. Continue with questions in #14.

Celebrations and Completions: This refers to the problem or singling out a student for outstanding work without embarrassing or violating the norms of that individual's group.

16) **Student acknowledgement**. You wanted to reward or acknowledge a student but weren't sure how. What were the specific circumstances? What were the alternative ways of acknowledgment that you considered? How did the individual respond to the celebration? How did others in your class and/or school respond?

STRUCTURE OF A CASE.

First, describe your problem, identifying who you — the author — are. Next, provide some context for your case (type of school, students, community). Then write as vivid an account as you can. Specifically indicate if/when the cultural or ethnic background of students had played an important part in your teaching intervention or practice. When appropriate, end your case with some unresolved questions.

In a second section, briefly reflect back on your narrative. If a similar situation should occur again, would you do anything differently? Why?

The best cases are written with some dramatic quality. The problems are written so that readers will identify immediately with the teacher who confronts the problem and will want to know what happened. Don't worry about the quality of your writing in the first draft. You will have opportunities to revise your case.

Length. Your case should be between one and three double-spaced typed pages long. When in doubt, write more rather than less. It is always easier to delete information than add to it.

Commentary. Remember, your case will be commented on by other experienced educators. Try to describe your dilemma so that our commentators will have something substantive to discuss.

LC 3731 .D59 1993

Diversity in the classroom

DATE DUE			
APR 2 0 1998			
NOV 1 1 2000			

CONCORDIA UNIVERSITY LIBRARY
2811 NE Holman St.
Portland, OR 97211